Remembering Paradise Park

 UNIVERSITY PRESS OF FLORIDA

Florida A&M University, Tallahassee
Florida Atlantic University, Boca Raton
Florida Gulf Coast University, Ft. Myers
Florida International University, Miami
Florida State University, Tallahassee
New College of Florida, Sarasota
University of Central Florida, Orlando
University of Florida, Gainesville
University of North Florida, Jacksonville
University of South Florida, Tampa
University of West Florida, Pensacola

Remembering

PARADISE PARK

Tourism and Segregation at Silver Springs

Lu Vickers and Cynthia Wilson-Graham

University Press of Florida

Gainesville · Tallahassee · Tampa · Boca Raton

Pensacola · Orlando · Miami · Jacksonville · Ft. Myers · Sarasota

A Florida Quincentennial Book

Library of Congress Control Number: 2015933804
ISBN 978-0-8130-6152-8

The University Press of Florida is the scholarly publishing agency for the State
University System of Florida, comprising Florida A&M University, Florida Atlantic
University, Florida Gulf Coast University, Florida International University, Florida
State University, New College of Florida, University of Central Florida, University
of Florida, University of North Florida, University of South Florida, and University
of West Florida.

University Press of Florida
15 Northwest 15th Street
Gainesville, FL 32611-2079
http://www.upf.com

To the memory of Mr. Eddie Leroy Vereen and his loving family

—LU VICKERS

To my mother, the late Juanita Wilson-Bernard, and father,
Lemuel E. Walker Sr., Johnnie C. Bernard Jr., and other families
who experienced segregation and discrimination

—CYNTHIA WILSON-GRAHAM

Paradise Park

Take a day off, but don't play dice.
Leave your bad habits home and try to be nice,
What? Haven't you heard the good news yet?
Well I don't gamble, but I'll give you a bet.
I don't play cards and I don't shoot crap
But if you don't know, you must be a sap.
Bring a bathing suit, not an evening gown.
In the middle of Florida, there's a little Indian town, Ocala!
You said it, come on down
Turn off highway four hundred forty-one,
Don't drive too fast, you're facing the sun.
You go dead east from the Old Coast Line.
Don't miss a chance to have a good time,
You'll see the sign, turn off, now
Where the road is lime, and before you know it
You'll say sublime!
Paradise is Marion County's colored park
You'll see so much when you come to the mark
You'll want to ask somebody is this Noah's Ark?
You'll find a pavilion, and a fawn or two.
Someone will guide you, you're welcome, don't fret
You're near the water, but your feet ain't wet.
Wait till I tell you, now all set
You can cruise down Silver River, in a boat you choose.
You'll want plenty comfort, so wear old shoes,
You'll see so many wonders, you'll tell all the news.
You'll have lots of fun, if you listen to me.
I'll name just a few things I want you to see.
The Devil's kitchen and the Christmas tree.
See the fish play ball, one two and three
Park Paradise on Silver River
You'll agree with me is the place to be.
When the day is over, you will dance with joy
Fill your pockets with money
Yes, do that my boy!
Bring your brown gal to Wonder River
You don't need a fine car,
Just an old flivver.
The water is so clear it looks like ice.
You said it old pal, it's Park Paradise.

Minnie A. L. Dickerson, *The Struggle for Survival: A Partial History of the Negroes of Marion County, 1865–1976*

SILVER SPRINGS
FROM
PARADISE PARK
FOR COLORED PEOPLE

SILVER SPRINGS
FROM
PARADISE PARK
FOR COLORED PEOPLE

ENJOY WORLD'S MOST FASCINATING GLASS BOTTOMED BOAT RIDE OVER THE CRYSTAL CLEAR WATERS OF SILVER SPRINGS

Contents

Posing in their swimsuits in an advertisement for Paradise Park
are (*left to right*) Ida Lee Donaldson, unknown, Susie Long, Alma
Jacobs, Patricia Bright, and Ernestine Stevenson, 1950. Photo by
Bruce Mozert. By permission of Bruce Mozert. Courtesy of Cynthia
Wilson-Graham.

1

Paradise Park at Silver Springs

~~~~~~

If it's in there, it'll come out some old day. Like the water in the
underground cave like Silver Springs. Underground for nobody knows
. . . how many centuries of years, to break through in that crystal clear
spring at last. That's the way life is, when you come to think about it.
Some folks are surface water and are easily seen and known about.
Others get caught underground, and have to cut and gnaw their way
out if they ever get seen by human eyes.

ZORA NEALE HURSTON, *SERAPH ON THE SUWANNEE*

In 1948, one year before Paradise Park was created as a recreation area
"for colored people only" by Carl Ray and William "Shorty" Davidson,
the owners of Silver Springs, Zora Neale Hurston published those
words about the spring in *Seraph on the Suwannee*, her only novel
about "Florida crackers." Her character Jim is explaining the nature
of water to Arvay, his wife. The words could well be used to describe
what has happened to the history of Paradise Park, just downriver
from Silver Springs, one of Florida's oldest attractions. Not the memories—they live on in people who visited the park—but the history.
The words that get written down. The history of Silver Springs glided
along the surface of the Silver River for all to see, while the story of
her darker sister remained underground. Same water, different story.
But water knows no color, as a young Johnnye Jacobs pointed out
to her mother back in the 1950s while swimming at Paradise Park:
"Mama, don't they know we're swimming in the same water and riding on the same boats?"[1]

At the time Johnnye Jacobs asked her mother that question, Silver Springs was one of the biggest tourist attractions in the country.

As Florida historian and photographer Gary Monroe recently said, it "was the Disney World of its Day—Florida's premiere tourist attraction."[2] Nineteenth-century visitors included Ulysses S. Grant, Thomas Edison, and Mary Todd Lincoln, who traveled by steamboat up the Ocklawaha River to the spring. By the early 1930s filmmakers discovered that it was the perfect spot for making movies like the Tarzan series, *The Yearling*, and *Creature of the Black Lagoon*, featuring Ricou Browning in the underwater scenes as the Gill Man. Browning also worked on about a third of the one hundred episodes of the 1960s television show *Seahunt* starring Lloyd Bridges that were filmed at Silver Springs.[3] Three James Bond movies featured scenes filmed at the spring: *Moonraker*, *Thunderball*, and *Never Say Never Again*. Arlene Francis staged her television show there; Ray and Davidson named a glass bottom boat after her. Silver Springs was also home to the internationally famous herpetologist Ross Allen, who established his Reptile Institute on site in 1929 and began managing the Silver Springs Seminole Indian Village in 1935. Allen did serious research with antivenom, but he also wrestled alligators and anacondas and milked rattlesnakes. Tommy Bartlett brought in his International Deer Ranch, and various other attractions were added over the years. Located in Ocala, Florida, Silver Springs attracted around 1.5 million visitors a year during its heyday from the 1950s to the late 1960s. Most were drawn there by an unprecedented advertising campaign that included traveling dioramas and billboards featuring its "World Famous Glass Bottom" boats captained exclusively by African Americans.

The tourism boom began during World War II, when the attraction targeted members of the armed forces who came to Florida to train. This campaign pulled in about 200,000 servicemen and women, and Silver Springs won an award for "wartime publicity and advertising." Growth continued in the postwar era when Ray and Davidson bombarded hotels and motels with free "doormats and mileage meters" featuring Silver Springs.[4] One year the advertising team plastered five thousand "See Silver Springs" arrows throughout the South.[5] It didn't hurt that on hand was Bruce Mozert, legendary photographer of Silver Springs, making kitschy photos of girls cavorting underwater and on land to send out to newspapers. It also didn't hurt that the postwar era kicked off the age of automobile travel and paid vacations. Visitors to Silver Springs quadrupled after the war.[6] Some of those lured there during this period were African Americans. They were turned away because at that time, segregation was in full force, either by law or custom, not just in Florida but across the United States from coast to coast.

Roosevelt Faison of Ft. McCoy, a small town that originated during the Seminole Wars, became a glass bottom boat captain at Silver Springs in 1956, one year after *Revenge of the Creature of the Black Lagoon* was filmed there. In 2014 he celebrated his fifty-eighth year of working on the river. "At that time there wasn't an admission," he said of the early days at the attraction. "You could just walk in. You didn't even have to pay for parking. You'd just drive in, and African Americans could do that, and they probably wouldn't be confronted if they came in and milled around the park. But the minute they started to go onto any ride or any place like that, then they would be confronted. If they were in the park just looking around, they probably wouldn't run up on anything, but if they walked up to the glass bottom boat ticket office and said, 'I want a ticket for the boat or for the jungle cruise or for Ross Allen,' that's when they would be told. That's why they opened Paradise Park."[7]

To their credit, during an era when swimming pools, lakes, and even beaches on the Atlantic Ocean were hard to come by for African Americans, Carl Ray and Shorty Davidson turned to Eddie Vereen, a Silver Springs boat captain, not only to manage Paradise Park

Above: Eddie Leroy Vereen and his wife, Fannie, stand before their family. The caption on the photo says it all: "The best family there is. My family." By permission of Reginald Lewis.

Left: Eddie Leroy Vereen was asked to come and work at Silver Springs by Carl Ray and Shorty Davidson. He became a boat captain and later was asked to help develop Paradise Park. This photograph was made at Silver Springs before he went to Paradise Park. By permission of Reginald Lewis.

but essentially to create it from the ground up using their resources. Vereen was born in the town of Silver Springs in 1897 and grew up along the Silver River. "My grandfather was the second oldest of five children," said Reginald Lewis. "Their home was next to creek to the east of Paradise Park. In fact, the cane patch in Tommy Bartlett's Deer Ranch up at Silver Springs was part of my great-grandfather's land. My grandfather was working as a mechanic at a Buick garage in Ocala and had a reputation as an outstanding worker. Ray and Davidson offered him a job as a boat captain, and then they chose him to help open and manage Paradise Park."[8] Vereen and his brother David had attended the one-room schoolhouse in Silver Springs, and on some afternoons their father Henry would pick them up and take them down to the river to where the paddleboat *Ocklawaha* docked. There the boys would dive into the water to collect coins tossed in by the tourists, often raking in more cash in a day than their father did in a month. Vereen began driving a glass bottom boat at Silver Springs in 1946.[9]

He was the perfect person to manage Paradise Park, according to his daughter Henrietta "Chippie" Vereen Cunningham. "My daddy was at Paradise Park by birth and by choice," she told a reporter in 2005. "He was born there—his home site being just down the springs a bit. But it was by choice that he helped open Paradise Park. Why? Because it was the right thing to do at the time."[10]

Luresa Lake, interviewed in 2013 for this book at age eighty-four, worked as a model at Paradise Park in the late 1940s and '50s, posing for photographer Bruce Mozert, who used her image on postcards and in brochures that were sent around the world. Some of the photos were made at Silver Springs. She never understood how a natural attraction like a spring ended up being segregated. "I always wondered why the white people decided they needed to separate Silver Springs, which was meant for the world to see, but they separated it from the black folks. It wasn't right. The whole place should have been open to everybody for a lifetime. No one should have the right to separate water and the facilities like that." She pointed out an additional affront that came with segregation: "The glass bottom boats we used, they used them too, but we'd have to call them if black people wanted to ride up and down the river. Years ago that's the way it was. When

Paradise Park was made, we thanked God that we could go at all. And that's what happened."[11]

Faison agreed. "It's the way times were," he said. "Young people don't understand segregation, but if you lived through those times, it was the way of life. I worked [at Silver Springs], but if I wanted my family to go on the boat, I had to go down [to Paradise Park]. Yet and still, I entertained them up here. You thought about it, but at the time, that's the way life was, and you just lived with it. They had signs that said 'Colored' on the bathrooms. Blacks could come here, but then they would really encourage them to go to Paradise Park. A lot of times they would even try to get some of us to go out there and tell them to go to Paradise Park, guys from the yard, the parking lot."[12]

One of the people turned away from Silver Springs was Carl Chancellor, who won a 1994 Pulitzer Prize for a series in the *Akron Beacon* about race and who subsequently became editorial director for Center for American Progress, a nonpartisan educational group. He was one of those African American tourists who went to Silver Springs before it was desegregated and was told he couldn't come in at the "whites only entrance." A *New York Times* reporter wrote that Chancellor recalled "being one of only a handful of passengers on the blacks' boat, while whites crowded onto a boat that looked full enough to capsize."[13]

Just days after Paradise Park opened, Martin Andersen, publisher of the *Orlando Sentinel*, told a group of Marion County officials that if they wanted Ocala to be as big as St. Petersburg, they need not look further than the springs: "The secret of Ocala's potential growth and the secret of Ocala's possibilities lies in Silver Springs." However, he continued, "Your problem is to grab those million people who every year come to visit Silver Springs and who spend a million dollars at that spot every year. Suppose you held them here three days instead of three hours?" He ended his comments by telling the crowd that on two recent occasions he had spoken to President Truman; the two men talked about Silver Springs.[14] Just one year earlier, Truman had issued Order 8801 to desegregate the armed forces and the federal Civil Service, and although he hadn't achieved all his goals regarding desegregation, he had "done more than any President since Lincoln to awaken the American conscience to the issues of Civil Rights."[15]

A group of scouts watch their friends feeding the fish from the glass bottom boat. Photo by Bruce Mozert. By permission of Bruce Mozert. Courtesy of Marion County Black Archives.

Shorty David-son, who owned Silver Springs with Carl Ray, speaks to a crowd at Paradise Park. Photo by Bruce Mozert. By permission of Bruce Mozert. Courtesy of Cynthia Wilson-Graham.

After Andersen left, Shorty Davidson spoke. "I am sorry that Martin Andersen isn't here, because I want to tell him to tell Harry we now have a place to take care of his negroes," he said, referring to Paradise Park.[16] Davidson's statement that they opened Paradise Park to "take care of" Truman's "negroes" was less altruistic than he made it out to be, according to Henry Jones, former lifeguard, boat driver, and bottle collector at the park and Eddie Vereen's nephew. He seconded what Faison said, adding that Ray and Davidson did not create Paradise Park purely to accommodate African American tourists who stopped by on their way elsewhere; they also created Paradise Park to answer the demands of the African American boat drivers. "Paradise Park was a necessity to cut down on people wanting to go to Silver Springs, including the family and friends of boat drivers," he said. "My mom was a school teacher in Sparr, and her brother Uncle Eddie[Vereen] drove a glass bottom boat. What Uncle Eddie would do in the winter time was cut the back way from Sparr to Silver Springs. The kids had to be quiet. They would start from the second spot and Uncle Eddie would load them onto the boat; they had to be really quiet. This was before Paradise Park. Other boat drivers would do it, then churches would want to come. It was getting kind of complicated, but they would do it and it was sneaky, and the kids couldn't scream. Yes, we were being abused. But when you grew up with it, you didn't feel it as much. Today the kids would beat somebody up. There used to be a concrete wall where they could load the boats. If the water was high enough, you could climb on the boats down where they parked them below the spring, but you couldn't walk on the sidewalks at Silver Springs. They just had to be quiet. The owners of Silver Springs would allow some of the boat drivers to take out family, but there were guidelines. Segregation was terrible. It was terrible. You weren't proud of that."[17]

With their resistance to being excluded from visiting the park where they worked, the Silver Springs boat captains seemed to be taking a page out of the history of another famous underground attraction. Mammoth Cave in Kentucky is the longest known cave system in the world and one of America's earliest and most popular tourist attractions, rivaled in its day only by Niagara Falls. Like Silver Springs, Mammoth Cave was a segregated attraction, although the workforce was not. Some of the first people to work at the cave were African American slaves, who were sent in to mine saltpeter, an ingredient used to produce gunpowder. By 1838 the demand for saltpeter diminished and Mammoth Cave became a tourist attraction, and the slaves and their descendants began to work as guides, "[opening] up the golden age of cave exploration for Mammoth Cave." They entertained visitors from around the world, including Ole Bull, a famous Norwegian violinist, Ralph Waldo Emerson, and George Armstrong Custer.[18]

In 1920 cave guide Matt Bransford, a descendant of Materson Bransford, one of the original guides, transformed his and his wife Zemmie's two-story home into a tourist lodge for African Americans, "[creating] a separate space for African American tourists on the periphery of a place patronized by white tourists," as historian Katie Algeo wrote. "The Bransford Hotel was probably not unique in this regard, but . . . it demonstrates that African Americans employed in the white tourism sector could, on occasion, facilitate African American access to these same attractions, subtly challenging the 'whites only' norm of white American tourism."[19] And like Matt Bransford, who traveled the country to invite African Americans to come and stay at his lodge and see Mammoth Cave, Eddie Vereen did the same for Paradise Park. Vereen was just one of the local African Americans who had lived, worked, and played at Silver Springs since the turn of the nineteenth century and who wanted their families, friends, and communities to see the spring that so astonished abolitionist Harriet Beecher Stowe when she drifted over it in the 1870s. She wrote that she felt she was

> floating through an immense cathedral where white marble columns meet in vast arches overhead and are reflected in the grassy depths below . . . the transparent depth of the water gave the impression that our boat was moving through the air. Every pebble and aquatic plant we glided over, seemed, in the torchlight, invested with prismatic brightness. What a sight was that! There is nothing on earth comparable to it!

Stowe was just as taken with the African American crew when they "[sang] their way through the book of Revelation," heading back down the Ocklawaha, the chorus of "De White Horse" echoing through the trees: "It was the call for soldiers for the last battle. . . . There was something thrilling and grand in these wild words, breathed into the

A group of visitors look out toward the float in the swimming area of Paradise Park. The boat dock is to the right. Photo by Bruce Mozert. By permission of Bruce Mozert.

Remembering Paradise Park

dark arches of the forest by these weird voices, singing as many parts as the birds and the wind . . . and these black men had showed on many a field they were 'not afeared to die.'"[20]

Although some of Florida's state parks set aside separate beaches for African Americans, Silver Springs was the only Florida roadside attraction that created a separate facility for African Americans. However, in the mid-1950s Curtis Bok wrote a letter to the American Foundation, which oversaw Bok Tower in Lake Wales, expressing his delight with changes made by Ken Morrison, the new manager: "The most extraordinary thing that he has done is to desegregate the rest rooms. Taking a fresh new look at the situation, he concluded that very few Negroes visit the Sanctuary and that most of the visitors are from the North." Bok added that Morrison "put up modest 'Men' and 'Women' only signs and sat back to see what would happen. Nothing has as yet."[21] A 1956 *Sarasota Herald Tribune* report on recreational facilities across the state found that most Florida cities had made only "token efforts" to meet the recreation needs of their African American residents. By then Paradise Park was hosting 100,000 visitors a year.[22]

Reginald Lewis helped bring in some of those visitors. Vereen put his whole family to work including Lewis, his grandson, who started working at the park when he was four years old, making fifty cents a week by pulling a wagon and picking up bottles; by the time he was twelve he was opening and closing the park. When he was eight, he was photographed by Leroy Roundtree, and his image was used on a Paradise Park advertisement that read: "No wonder I'm smiling! I've seen Silver Springs from the Glass Bottomed Boats at Florida's Paradise Park."[23] Paradise Park did not have its own fleet of boats; when enough people gathered, a dispatcher would call up to Silver Springs and have a boat sent down to carry them upriver. Ironically, according

Reginald Lewis, grandson of Eddie Vereen, was featured in one of the ink blotters advertising Paradise Park. Photo by Leroy Roundtree. Courtesy of Cynthia Wilson-Graham.

Eddie Vereen glances over the grounds of Paradise Park from the boat dock. Photo by Bruce Mozert. By permission of Bruce Mozert. Courtesy of Cynthia Wilson-Graham.

to Henry Jones, African American boat captain Bennie Smith's wife Doretha "sold every glass bottom ticket" at Silver Springs before integration, "because they thought she was white." Later, while still an employee of Silver Springs, she worked as an assistant to Vereen.[24]

The late Edgar Samuel, who drove boats at Silver Springs for twenty-eight years beginning in 1946, described going down to Paradise Park to pick up African American tourists. "William Pryor, William Crowell, and I used to run the pack of Vereen's volunteers," he said, referring to a couple of longtime glass bottom boat drivers. "We didn't go to the head of the springs," he said, referring to the actual grounds of Silver Springs, "and they didn't visit us at our end of the park, and to my knowledge no one ever tried to visit; that's just the way it was. Carl Ray was a very kind man; he treated his employees fair; however his partner Shorty Davidson was the opposite. [Walter C.] Buck Ray, Carl's son, was a kind man; when I needed something for my family he was always there for me. Buck Ray was always in my corner." Despite the kindness of the Rays, Samuel still felt the sting of segregation. "I always spoke up for what was right. I didn't like that we worked at Silver Springs but could not visit with our families, or use the bathrooms, or eat."[25]

Lewis told *Ocala Magazine* that Ray and Davidson sought out his grandfather to manage Paradise Park because of his "honesty, commitment to details, and because he genuinely loved people of all colors. My granddaddy was very humble, and he wanted everything to go right. If a family came to the park that didn't have money, he was known to take them out on a free boat ride to at least the first spring so they could experience it."[26] In another interview Lewis summed up his grandfather's legacy at the attraction: "The main reason people went to Paradise Park was because there was a warm personal touch to it. My grandfather patrolled that place like it was a kingdom."[27]

And what a kingdom it was. Ray and Davidson spared no expense in creating a beautiful landscape with swaying palm trees and lush flowerbeds. The late Timothy Green helped. He began working as a gardener at Silver Springs when he was a teenager in the early 1930s and recalled planting the horseshoe palms along the river that are featured in so many Silver Springs postcards. Later he helped Eddie Vereen build the foundation of Paradise Park, then worked there as a gardener too. "I just wanted Paradise Park to look just as 'good' as the Silver Springs park," he said.[28]

A white sand beach bordered the Silver River. Up under the shade trees were a gift shop, a soda fountain, and a pavilion complete with a "piccolo," better known these days as a jukebox. Picnic tables were first come, first served, and there was plenty of grass where friends could spread out a blanket. In 1956 Eddie Vereen bragged about Paradise Park to a reporter: "I have traveled to every Negro recreational facility in Florida and nowhere have I found a set-up to compare to what we have here."[29] Each Labor Day the local American Legion post would sponsor beauty contests, and each year there were Boy Scout encampments and Easter egg hunts and wade-in-the-water baptisms. Ross Allen's rattlesnakes were handled with care by Willie Johnson, J. D. Williams, and James Glover. Glass bottom boats glided over the catfish hotel and turtle meadows. Every Christmas, Timothy Howard donned his Santa Claus suit and arrived at the dock on a glass bottom boat with oranges for all. Spelling Bee champions and Queens for a

Timothy Howard, dressed as Santa Claus, arrived at Paradise Park on a glass bottom boat. Here he passes out Christmas gifts to the children. Eddie Vereen, wearing a hat, looks on. Photo by Bruce Mozert. By permission of Bruce Mozert. Courtesy of Marion County Black Archives.

Day were given trips to Paradise Park as their top prizes. It was a kingdom where white folks were not allowed, although one or two slipped in every now and then. It was a kingdom where catfish played football, flowers bloomed underwater, and alligators had so much fish to eat, a young man could swim without worry.

When Ray and Davidson sold Silver Springs to ABC in 1962, after nearly four decades of ownership and stewardship, Silver Springs itself began to "lose its local flavor and the support of the local government as a community." Leon Cheatom, a longtime employee at Silver Springs, told historian Thomas Berson that under ABC, the attraction no longer felt "like family." Ray and Davidson had always encouraged relatives of employees to apply for jobs, and it wasn't unusual to find that boat captains were cousins, or brothers, or that one of them was married to the ticket seller or kin to the groundskeepers. ABC was "more concerned with the bottom line and instilling a uniform, corporate environment," than with fostering improvements. Within the first few years of the new ownership Ross Allen was forced to sell the Reptile Institute he had owned since the late 1920s, and Tommy Bartlett was forced to sell his deer ranch. ABC also tried to homogenize the boatmen's presentations. Cheatom told Berson that Ray and Davidson had valued the captains' individual styles, but ABC actually brought in "speaking coaches . . . to help fine-tune the tour narratives the captains had spent decades crafting and honing," a move that squashed the colorful tales that brought in tips. Prior to ABC's arrival, said Cheatom, "People wanted folklore, and we gave it to them."[30]

Paradise Park suffered under ABC as well; its hours were cut back, and the beloved park finally closed in 1969, a bittersweet result not just of the corporate takeover but also of desegregation. Rather than consulting with the community or integrating the park into Silver Springs, ABC made a decision simply to shut it down, to gate and lock the road leading into the park. The swimming area is now fenced off and overgrown; the jukebox is gone. The concession stand and picnic tables were bulldozed into rubble along with the gift shop. Bits and pieces of broken crockery and soda bottles are scattered across the ground. The dock where patrons boarded the glass bottom boats for a trip up the Silver River to the spring is gone; the ladder from the swimming area lies twisted beneath the trees. The parking lot that once held tour buses and sedans from practically every state in the country is now a field of tall scraggly pines. The sign that welcomed visitors has oxidized to ash gray, the letters faded almost past recognition. Paradise Park has met a fate similar to that of the lettering on the sign—there is no mention of the attraction in histories of Silver Springs or Ocala beyond an occasional sentence or two. But the river runs on, and the park has remained very much alive in the hearts and

Leon Cheatom, also known as "Mr. Silver Springs," uncovers the side of a concrete park bench at the overgrown Paradise Park site. Photo by Cynthia Wilson-Graham. By permission of Cynthia Wilson-Graham.

minds of those who visited the popular attraction that opened on Emancipation Day in 1949.

One of the people baptized at Paradise Park was the late Rev. Dr. Mack King Carter, pastor emeritus at New Mount Olive Baptist Church in Fort Lauderdale, one of the largest African American churches in Florida. He told a reporter he rode to Ocala aged six, "wedged between his mother and grandmother . . . to become a member of the New Bethel Baptist Church." That meant wading into the Silver River from the sandy shores of the park for a baptism on an early Sunday morning in 1953.[31]

By the time Carter turned ten he was a deacon, known for his preaching. By the time he turned nineteen he was pastor at Calvary Baptist Church in Ocala. Noted for his scholarship and "oratorical prowess," Reverend Carter, when asked what he thought of Eddie Vereen's kingdom said, "[Paradise Park was] a 'Mass of Colored Association.'"[32]

When lifelong Ocala resident McCloud Raines was asked if he remembered or ever visited Paradise Park, he replied, "Visited! Remember! Do I remember Paradise Park? Yeah, I remember; that's the only place blacks had to go." Raines said he would see some of the finest and most beautiful women at Paradise Park, women from all over the

June Gary Hopps (*left*) and Faye Gary (*third from left*) pose with friends next to the azaleas on the grounds of Paradise Park. Photo by Bruce Mozert. By permission of Bruce Mozert. Courtesy of Marion County Black Archives.

Remembering Paradise Park

country. "You talkin' about beautiful black women—all you had to do was visit the park." He said the music would be playing; people would be dancing, and the children playing and swimming. His family didn't have a car to drive to the park, but that didn't stop him from going. "My friends and I would walk from Tucker Hill to Paradise Park at Silver Springs. There were not many cars on the road, like there are now. It didn't matter how many miles I had to walk; I just wanted to get to the park to have some fun." Silver Springs Boulevard was a dirt road at that time, he said; there was no pavement, so he would take short cuts to the park when he had to walk.[33]

Nathaniel "Pepper" Lewis, a former Silver Springs boat driver, remembered swimming at Paradise Park two or three times a week, sometimes walking there, other times hitching a ride with his uncle, another beloved Silver Springs boat captain. "My uncle, J. W.

Young people loved to sit on the lush green grass at Paradise Park enjoying the sites and each other. Photo by Bruce Mozert. By permission of Bruce Mozert. Courtesy of Cynthia Wilson-Graham.

Paradise Park at Silver Springs

Culpepper, the one who raised me, used to drive a boat at the springs and he'd pick us up and give us a ride down the river. Paradise Park was a beautiful place. They had a beach there, and alligators would be sitting on the bank. I can't understand why they're eating people now, because we'd be swimming out there, and they'd just lay up on the bank and relax; I guess they had so much fish to eat, they didn't bother people."[34]

The story behind Lewis's uncle—"the one who raised me"—and his wife, Emma "Dolly" Lewis Culpepper, exemplifies the tight African American community in Ocala that made Paradise Park the family affair it was during its twenty years of existence. J. W. and Dolly took in Nathaniel and his three siblings after their father was killed in a sawmill accident in 1945. Before he passed away Hudson Lewis worried that his four children would be placed into foster care, because his young wife didn't have the resources to raise them. He summoned his sister Dolly to his bed and told her, "I'm going home . . . Dolly, please don't let them take my children. Keep them together. I want you to raise them." She and J. W. agreed and Nathaniel and his siblings headed to Tucker Hill, where they grew up and where Dolly went on to become Ocala's "mother to the motherless," a woman worthy of her own Hollywood movie. She and her husband couldn't say no to children. "Every time we said, 'Let's have a baby,' they'd hand us another child," she told a reporter in 1998. "We didn't have time to have one of our own. I walked away from my own to help someone else, but I'm glad I did." In 1957, while Dolly was driving her husband to work, they were involved in an automobile accident and J. W. Culpepper was gravely injured. He passed away within the week. His wife went on to care for more than fifteen children over the years, including her last, Daunte Culpepper, who grew up to become a highly regarded quarterback in the National Football League.[35]

Looking over a photograph of a group of African American lifeguards who worked at Paradise Park as well as at the local segregated pool, Brenda Vereen pointed out her father, educator James Croskey, and his twin brother Edward (pictured in chapter 9). "They named the recreation center after Edward," she said. "He was director of recreation. He was over the lifeguards at the Hampton pool; we weren't allowed to go to the other pool. He trained the lifeguards."[36] Like the Culpeppers, Edward Croskey also embodied the spirit of this

community; he worked tirelessly to make sure the local children were well tended. "If you're going to run a recreation program," he told a reporter in 1956, "you can't just throw a ball at a bunch of kids and then go fishing. You're going to have to stay right there with them." And stay he did, prompting the director of Ocala's recreation department to observe, "Sometimes I think Eddie carries this entire program on his back."[37]

"I remember going to the park," Brenda said. "I was part of that growing up. I was born in the 1950s, and my daddy and my uncle would take me out there. All the holidays they'd have something big. I probably went every weekend because of my dad." She remembered riding the glass bottom boats and seeing the jungle cruise boats filled with white people. "We could go so far but we couldn't go up to the head spring until after integration. The jungle cruise would ride by and the people would wave at us. We'd jump off the dock. I was about

Crowds gather at the edge of the white sandy banks of the Silver River watching the children swim at Paradise Park. Photo by Bruce Mozert. By permission of Bruce Mozert. Courtesy of Marion County Black Archives.

Paradise Park at Silver Springs

The music from the "pic-colo" or jukebox entertained many guests as they danced in the pavilion at Paradise Park. Photo by Bruce Mozert. By permission of Bruce Mozert. Courtesy of Marion County Black Archives.

The Vereen family celebrates a birthday at their home. Eddie Vereen is seated at the rear right corner of the table with his grandson Reginald Lewis in his lap. Arizona Vereen-Turner is standing near the rear left corner. By permission of Henry Jones.

eight or nine then, and during my teenage years, it was the place to go for dancing."[38]

Brenda's cousin Carol Croskey said that from when she was about three to nine years old, Paradise Park was the place to be. "My fondest memories of Paradise Park," she said, "were the summer day trips to what I called a bandstand. There was a jukebox on that cement floor and it never stopped. I don't ever remember anybody putting money in it. Children and adults would be on the floor just dancing away. The two songs I always heard were 'The Twist' by Chubby Checker and 'Shotgun' by Jr. Walker and the All Stars, probably because there was a dance to go along with the song."[39] Reginald Lewis added that his grandfather kept that jukebox full of 45s except for "Annie Get Your Dog," which he didn't approve of. "He made Mr. Fuller come take it out. Mr. Fuller would come down and empty the box and add new records, and then he would drop a bunch of quarters in and the music would play and play. My cousin was out there on the dance floor doing a dance called 'The Dog' to Rufus Thomas's song 'Walk the Dog,' and my grandfather thought it was vulgar and told him not to do that. But later he told me, "Y'all think y'all have something; we had 'Pull the Mule.'"[40]

Henry Jones said he started working at the park when he was eleven. "I started out cleaning toilets. See, it opened in 1949 and I was born in '38. We always worked." He said despite or perhaps because of his uncle's strict rules, people felt completely at ease. "At Paradise Park, you could lay down wherever you wanted and nobody would bother you. Uncle Eddie had absolute control, and he ran it so well. We didn't realize how good it was till now. People would dance; some kids didn't go any further—they didn't go in the water, or picnic; they just danced. When it was time to close, you didn't question him. He was straight up, in control. He wasn't mean, but you didn't question him; he was tough."[41]

Sylvia Jones is Eddie Vereen's niece and Henry's sister. She started working at the park when she was five years old. "Uncle Eddie was a good businessman and he managed Paradise Park with professional expertise. He did it all: public relations, sales, personnel, always with the help of his administrative assistant, and main cashier, Ms. Doretha Smith."

Mattie Johnson serves customers from the concession stand at Paradise Park. Photo by Bruce Mozert. By permission of Bruce Mozert. Courtesy of Marion County Black Archives.

Sylvia's memories of Paradise Park are vivid. "You could smell the hamburgers," she said. She too remembered the dance floor. "They would dance to the music out of the jukebox, the now old-fashioned kind, spinning 45s," she said of the teenagers who visited the park. "You may have gone and gotten your swim trunks and the rubber I.D. tag to put on your ankle to show you'd paid for swimming and a claim basket for your personal belongings, and you'd be dancing, and the music got so good . . . and it'd get all heated up in there, and Uncle Eddie would come along and say 'God night' and he'd go over there and unplug the jukebox. He was very stern. He did not use profanity and he didn't allow it at the park from anybody, including visitors."[42] Henry added that "God night" was one of the exclamations he used instead of cursing. "He also said 'Shotgun,' when he got mad. It was the same as cussing," he said. "You didn't mess with him then."[43]

Johnnye Jacobs and Doris Jacobs-Smith both remembered that Eddie Vereen didn't play around. "If you swore," Johnnye said, "he would turn that jukebox off. It was over. He was really strict. You couldn't even play the radio around him."[44] Doris agreed. "If you said something ugly you would have to go. He was training people up the way they ought to go—that's what that was."[45]

Arizona Vereen-Turner said that family or not, her uncle expected them to work hard. He ran the concessions at the park, earning the proceeds. "We couldn't take a break 'cause our uncle would get on the loudspeaker and tell us our break was over," she said, laughing. "We didn't make no money." But then she added, "Our cousin Ron called him Papa." She said she "mostly worked in the gift shop and the swimming shop; they had a number and they'd get that basket. They had t-shirts, and flags and snow globes, all kinds of things: back scratchers and pencils. I talked to someone who said they had a Paradise Park pennant." She said sometimes when she had a free moment she would hit the dance floor until she heard her uncle's voice. "I liked to dance, and they'd have to call me back to work."[46]

Vereen may have had a firm hand, but he was clearly loved by his family. "Everyone called him Papa," said Reginald. "My kids tried to call me Papa and I wouldn't let them. There was only one Papa in our family."[47] Lewis told a reporter that one afternoon his grandfather mentioned that he would like some fish, so Lewis headed out to the dock and went to work. Because the Silver Springs owners didn't allow fishing during the day, he had to hide what he was doing, so he sat down, tied a line to his toe and sank the baited hook into the water. A bass hit the bait and the knot tightened on his toe, nearly slicing it off, but he was not deterred. When boat captain Sammie Cheatom pulled up to check on him, he didn't want to get into trouble and he acted as if he were okay. Somehow he managed to keep his toe, land the fish, and present it to his grandfather.[48]

In 2003 when the City of Ocala renamed a part of the street where he lived Eddie Leroy Vereen Court, one of his six biological children, Henrietta "Chippie" Vereen Cunningham, said "My daddy deserves it. He was an ordinary citizen, but he did extraordinary activities on behalf of mankind and humanity. I am so pleased the city agreed to honor him in such a distinguished and magnificent way."[49] She still lives in their original home, where her father maintained an

extraordinary life. In addition to his own six children, he took in two of his sister's children after she passed away and then made sure each of his own children as well as the children he took in went to college. His support didn't stop there. "Uncle Eddie was very supportive of my grandmother's determination to further her education. She used to speak of days when she would walk six miles to school. She went to Bethune-Cookman College under the teaching of Mary McLeod Bethune for two years and from there to Florida A&M to finish her bachelor's degree. Mary Vereen Jones was an educator in Marion County for over forty-three years.

"Uncle Eddie married Aunt Fannie after Aunt Carrie, his first wife, died, and they remodeled this house," said Sylvia. "We had a hammock in the house before it was remodeled and we'd lie on the porch, swinging and sleeping. This is the same house. Uncle Fordham, who was Aunt Fannie's brother, remodeled it." Looking over old family photos, she explained, "This is my grandmother. That's who raised me. Her name is Mary Louise Vereen Jones. There's Uncle Eddie in the back with a cigar. That's his brother Herbert; that's his brother Arthur; that's his brother David; that's Mary; she was the only girl living. They had two sisters and one brother who died: Cora, Hattie, and Strozier. You have to understand, the Vereens were born and raised in Silver

Springs," she said as she thumbed through the images. "That's one of me and Cynthia at Paradise Park; that's a picture of me at Paradise Park; that's a picture of some cousins at Paradise Park.

"Uncle Eddie made special Christmas cards. On the front of the cards would be Santa Claus on the glass bottom boat coming down the river with kids, and I always enjoyed that picture opportunity. Even though the Christmas cards were black and white, Mama dressed me in red and white. All of the children would be cute and Mr. Timothy Howard, one of the two black deputy sheriffs in Marion County, would be Santa Claus each year. I used to go down the river on the boat with Santa Claus—the sand was white, the water was so pretty and crystal clear. It was lovely. You could see the whole park." Sylvia pointed out that the pear and pecan trees in the backyard of the house were there when she was a child, and the kitchen was the "same kitchen Aunt Fannie cooked mustard greens in. Everybody loved Aunt Fannie's greens and dumplings."[50]

Ron McFadden and Cynthia Vereen are among the children visiting Santa Claus (Tim Howard) on his glass bottom boat. The *Walter Ray* is named after the son of Silver Springs owner Carl Ray. The photo was made into a Christmas card. By permission of Reginald Lewis.

Vivian Vereen Tillman, one of Vereen's daughters, now lives in Brunswick, Georgia, but still considers Ocala her home. Her husband was Eugene Tillman, a Georgia state representative. "My daddy was the manager of Paradise Park," she said. "Everything was in order; he wasn't a man of education—he didn't finish high school—but he was a smart, smart man. He drove a boat at Silver Springs and out of all those men there they picked him to be the manager. He had our car and he put the sign on it and he went from city to city from state to state. And busloads of people came."[51] Some days there would be more than 170 buses parked side by side in the parking lot, mostly from Florida and south Georgia. Vereen had attached the sign to the top of his 1947 Chevy, and as Sheryl Murphy wrote, he was "paid eight cents a mile whenever he had the sign on his car advertising Paradise Park and the car didn't move without the sign!"[52]

One of the people who came to Paradise Park was Dr. Dorsey Miller, a longtime political activist who helped start Ocala's NAACP Youth Council in the 1960s and who chaired the Florida Black Republicans for years before leaving the party. He grew up in Ocala. "A friend and I used to ride our bikes to Paradise Park . . . we were out there all the time. And when it closed, I felt the loss. I never had a desire to go on the other side, Silver Springs. It was different, you see. At Paradise Park, under the pavilion, we had what we used to call a 'piccolo.' We used to play records, dance and have a good time. We'd have picnics and socialize with each other. Those who wanted to swim could. We had some ownership in Paradise Park. Paradise Park was ours, we thought. We knew who owned it, but it was ours. We could go to Paradise Park and socialize and interact without making any excuses and without feeling as if we were guests. Paradise Park was home for us, just as Silver Springs was home for whites. After integration, we were not made to feel welcome. All of our traditions were lost. After I had children, I went over to Silver Springs to ride the glass bottom boat, and it was just altogether different. It was like being a guest in my own home. I never went back again."[53]

David Rackard, who at nineteen was vice president of the Ocala NAACP, got arrested several times for his civil rights work in the 1960s. He was also Eddie Vereen's cousin. "Oh, yes. I visited Paradise Park; my uncle Robert Wilson was a lifeguard out there. They called him 'Dukes.' I enjoyed it. I went out there all the time to swim. I was a

Boy Scout, and we used to have trips out there. Mr. Florence was my troop leader; he was also science teacher at Howard High." R. V. Florence was scout master of Troop 231 of the Marion Division of Negro Boy Scouts, and he was but one of the many community leaders who volunteered his time. Several of the men who committed to work with the Scouts also worked at Paradise Park: L. S. Tyson, Doc Smith, J. T. Glover, and Edward Croskey. The Negro Boy Scout troops had annual Paradise Park encampments beneath the trees in a field at the park.[54]

The Boy Scouts of America never openly sanctioned racial discrimination, but they did so tacitly, allowing local troops to determine whether they would integrate or not. In 1950 although "white and colored scout leaders" met at Covenant Missionary Baptist Church to discuss, among other things, recruiting more "Negro" scouts, the Marion County scouts joined segregated troops.[55] Former Eagle Scout Ross Allen opened his famous Reptile Institute at Silver Springs in 1929, and in 1957 he began hosting a yearly camporee for white scouts on Paradise Road down from Silver Springs. Ray and Davidson had provided Allen with a piece of land along the road, and scouting officials helped clear the fifty-acre tract for a campsite.[56]

Paradise Park at Silver Springs   27

A group of Boy Scouts from Troop 41, Bethlehem Baptist Church in Sarasota, pose for a picture while visiting Paradise Park. Photo by Bruce Mozert. By permission of Bruce Mozert. Courtesy of Marion County Black Archives.

From teenaged dancers to preachers performing mass baptisms to boy scouts enjoying a campout, Paradise Park was woven into the fabric of African American life in Marion County. When asked if she had gone to Paradise Park back in the day, Virginia Ferguson, the first African American woman boat captain at Silver Springs, laughed loudly. Then she grew dead serious. "Well, that was the only place *to* go," she said. "Being black, that was the only place to go. Where were you going, you know? During those days—you don't understand it—but that's all we had. It wasn't that we felt so bad about it; we appreciated what we had and really and truly, we'd love to have some of it back. That's what we had and that's what we enjoyed and it was something really, really wonderful."[57]

A large crowd gathers at Paradise Park. The swimming area is visible in the background. Photo by Bruce Mozert. By permission of Bruce Mozert. Courtesy of Marion County Black Archives.

2

Seminoles and African Americans in Marion County

There we were, a gouty old fellow and a girl of twenty in the wilderness of a Florida Pine forest with a surly Indian-Negro for our sole guide, philosopher and friend.

CHARLES DUNNING

Look heah you cake walkers, y'all oughter git up and limber up yo' joints. I heard them folks over to St. Augustine been oiling up wid goose grease, and over to Ocala, they been rubbing down in Snake oil.

ZORA NEALE HURSTON, *COLOR STRUCK*

There is no record of Zora Neale Hurston going to Paradise Park, but from her description of Silver Springs in *Seraph on the Suwannee*, and of those folks "over to Ocala" and their use of snake oil, she may well have wandered over to the park to watch James Glover or Willie Johnson milk snakes for the crowds at Paradise. Eatonville, her hometown, is only one and half hours south of the springs, and although Silver Springs was no Eatonville, in some ways it makes sense that Silver Springs would be the only Florida roadside attraction to open a separate park for African Americans. There is a long history of people of color in Marion County.

The area's earliest inhabitants were the Timucua Indians, who considered Silver Springs a "sacred shrine" and home to their "water gods." Then the Spanish invaded, Pánfilo de Narváez in 1528 and Hernando de Soto in 1539, and drove them out. A succession of Native American tribes followed: the Yemassee, Mikasuki, and Muskogee, along with the Creek tribes collectively known as the Seminoles.[1] In the early 1800s large numbers of escaped Gullah slaves made their way from southern coastal plantations of South Carolina and Georgia to Florida, where they found refuge with the Seminoles, living, inter-marrying, and later fighting as comrades in arms during the Seminole Wars, including battles at Fort King, just outside Ocala. In 1821, when the United States took possession of Florida after the first Seminole War, which Andrew Jackson called an "Indian and Negro War," Marion County's population was largely made up of Seminoles, Black Seminoles, and African Americans.[2]

A young warrior at the time, Osceola famously stood up amidst a group of Seminole chiefs at an 1834 meeting with U.S. government officials who planned to force the Florida Seminoles to relocate out West. He is said to have thrust his knife into the treaty shouting: "Am I a Negro? A slave? My skin is dark, but not black! I am an Indian, a Seminole. The white man shall not make me black. I will make the white man red with blood, and then blacken him in the sun and rain, where the wolf shall gnaw his bones and the buzzard shall live on his flesh."[3]

One of the most famous Black Seminoles who lived in what would become Marion County was Negro Abraham, a former slave to the Spaniards, who joined the Seminoles and became Chief Micanopy's slave. Once his skill as an interpreter became clear, Micanopy freed him and anointed Abraham as his "sense bearer" or advisor. Abraham participated in the Dade Massacre, which took place as U.S. troops were headed to Fort King (Ocala) to serve as reinforcements in the effort to remove the Seminoles, and which triggered the second Seminole War.[4]

The last remaining Seminoles were driven out when James Rogers purchased the land around the headwaters in 1845 while Florida was still a territory. White people then began to move into the area in larger numbers; by 1870 freed African Americans constituted a 73 percent majority in Marion County, and many of them had acquired land from their former owners around Silver Springs.[5] As Louis Chazal and Eloise Ott point out in *Ocali Country*, "There was less segregation of the races in Ocala in the last three decades of the Nineteenth Century and the first decade of the new century than now seems possible."[6] That togetherness did not last.

Peggy Mixon visits the Seminoles at Ross Allen's Seminole Indian Village at Silver Springs. Photo by Bruce Mozert. By permission of Peggy Mixon.

Ken Breslauer, historian and artifact collector, described the change that came about after Reconstruction and that persisted into the age of modern tourism: "Florida was one of the most segregated states. The attractions wanted everyone's money but didn't want to turn off whites," he said, referring to the decision to open Paradise Park.[7] The Seminoles suffered a different fate. In the new configuration of Florida as a place to attract tourists, Henry Coppinger Jr., the self-described "second white man born in the city of Miami," invented alligator wrestling, which then became synonymous with the Seminoles. He also opened one of the first "Indian Villages" in the state.[8] Then in 1934 Seminoles who had been forced out of the Marion County area were invited back to Silver Springs when Charles Metzger opened a "Seminole Village" on the bank of the Silver River with the help of about four Seminoles, who built the chickees and other structures that would form the village. Around sixty Seminoles moved to Ocala from the Big Cypress area, close by Immokalee. According to David Cook, who visited the attraction, the relationship between management and Seminoles quickly soured, and several families decided to live away from the eyes of the tourists.[9] Just one year after it opened, Ross Allen took over. Or, as former director of education at Silver Springs

Richard Martin described it in *Eternal Spring*, the "Mikasuki Seminoles returned to Silver Springs in 1935 establishing a colony under the direction of Ross Allen."[10] However, the Silver Springs Seminole Indian Village was no colony; it was a tourist attraction, and half a million people streamed through to watch the Seminoles go about their daily lives. To find an equally offensive setup for African Americans, tourists would have to drive an hour south of Ocala to Brooksville.

"The place that was really horrible, looking back, was Old Lewis Plantation," said Breslauer of the attraction that opened in Brooksville in the 1930s."[11] Lewis Plantation was a former turpentine plantation owned by Pearce Lewis, who turned it into a tourist attraction after demand for spirits of turpentine declined. He hired African Americans to play every stereotype in the book. The attraction was as offensive as a place could be, but no one seemed to care, as evidenced by this tidbit in a newspaper: "No neon signs herald this scene of two fast disappearing phases of Florida life, turpentine distilleries, and the Negro 'feudal' system which prevailed following the close of the Civil War."[12] Another piece described how Blanche Bruins, who lived on the plantation for over a decade, "dressed in typical 'Mammy' fashion," while she drove white tourists on a mule cart past little children playing in dusty yards, then on through acres of pine trees.[13] There was no mention of what she did or who she was during her days off.

The Seminoles at Silver Springs did their best to take advantage of their situation, adopting some of the tourist-luring devices that had been developed by tribes at other Indian tourist "villages"—including those opened by tribes themselves—such as making totem poles, drums, and leather moccasins to sell to the white visitors.[14] In a short film on the village at Silver Springs, it is clear how inhumane that life was: the camera pans over a couple of children playing, two women grinding corn, and Francis Osceola putting an alligator to sleep. A crowd of white people lean against a fence looking on curiously.[15] Mabel Bowers, who lived on the Hollywood reservation and sold dolls to a "commercial camp," described the various Indian villages across the state: "The white man owned the Indian Village and made a show out of the Indians. The whites would pay and go in and see how Indians lived, how they sleep on platforms, wrestle alligators. That's what they used to have, three or four of them in Miami."[16] Some of these villages

A Seminole woman makes clothes at the Seminole Indian Village at Silver Springs. By permission of Lu Vickers.

still exist today. However, as one historian observed, "both tourists and the Seminoles are aware that the Indians who populate the village chickees during the day go home to suburban style ranch homes at night."[17]

In 1939 Chief Osceola returned to the Silver Springs attraction in the form of a statue depicting his defiance of the white invasion. Osceola faced racism even when cast in stone. In a 1939 interview Bernice West, the sculptor, explained her fascination with the famous chief's resistance: "Perhaps it was because he was one-fourth white, Osceola was remarkably intelligent and though he possessed the characteristic Indian cunning, he was honest and upright."[18] The statue is said to have been erected on the very spot where Osceola plunged his knife into the treaty.

International scholar Dr. Joyce Hope Scott grew up in Santos, a small town outside Ocala, and remembered going to Paradise Park. She has been awarded two Fulbright scholarships in addition to many other awards and is now an associate professor of American Studies at Wheelock College in Boston. In a recent essay she commented on the legacy passed down by those pioneering families: "The Ocala area boasts an impressive history of African American communities and families. As African Americans in the area received news of Emancipation, they bought land, established churches, businesses and private schools (Fessenden and Howard Academies) and organized women's and men's philanthropic clubs." When Scott left home to pursue studies of the Harlem Renaissance, she wrote, she read authors who "recognized that language cannot be separated from power" and realized that Ocala had already taught her that lesson: "Indeed, in Ocala, Florida, I learned my first and most lasting lessons about language, power and identity."[19]

As noted earlier, the power of the African American identity in this community was one of the underlying reasons Ray and Davidson decided to open Paradise Park. This was a community that was not going to be denied access to one of the largest artesian springs in the world, and as Scott pointed out, the roots of this determination run all the way back to Emancipation. A freed slave, M. A. Clouts, became the first African American sheriff in 1868, and in the years that followed, seven African Americans were elected to the Florida legislature, including Samuel Small, Birch Gibson, and Singleton Coleman. Not only were blacks and whites legislating together; they also worshiped together until 1867, when Samuel Small and a group of former slaves departed from the predominantly white First Baptist church and created the Mount Moriah Baptist Church.[20] Members of Mount Moriah would later be among those who held baptisms at Paradise Park.

"A Negro Wedding down South—Ocala, Florida." The setting is Lincoln Heights, an African American neighborhood founded by Frank Gadson, who was an officer of the Metropolitan Savings Bank and manager of the Ocala Bazaar and Commercial Company. By permission of Wayne Nielsen.

A splinter church, Covenant Missionary Baptist, was led by Reverend O. V. Pinkston, who frequently contributed to programs at Paradise Park. He also allowed the NAACP Youth Council to hold its organizational meeting at Covenant Missionary Baptist Church and provided office and mass meeting space for the movement.[21] In 1964 Reverend Pinkston's son, Reverend Frank Pinkston Sr., became pastor of Mount Moriah. Historian Thelma Parker of Ocala later described Frank Pinkston as the "Liberator of Blacks of Marion County" for his leadership in the civil rights movement, risking his life to organize sit-ins at local businesses to bring on desegregation.[22] Still, even in the midst of his important and dangerous civil rights work, he took the time to enjoy Paradise Park with his family. A 1950s photograph shows the late Reverend Frank Pinkston holding his daughter at Paradise Park for a visit with Santa Claus.

By the early 1900s Marion County's African Americans were the most "prosperous [African Americans] in the South." The Ocala Bazaar and Commercial Company was owned by African Americans and patronized by both African Americans and whites. In 1891 the manager of the bazaar, Frank Gadson, was elected treasurer and tax collector of Ocala. He also sold real estate.[23] In a 1908 ad in the *Ocala Evening Star* he proclaims, "I have 60 choice residence lots in the blocks adjoining Howard Academy and Lincoln Heights." Lincoln Heights was a part of the Tucker Hill neighborhood.[24] Wayne Nielson came across a postcard depicting a "Negro Wedding in Lincoln Heights." He told a reporter in 2002 that the postcard made him realize what a rich African American history Ocala has. "It dawned on me that blacks at the turn of the century were excluded in history, and they had to carve out a niche for themselves, outside the mainstream."[25]

"In my nationwide search for the postcards, I was surprised to find many focused on the African-American community in Ocala," Nielson said recently. "These postcards provide a glimpse into a part of the segregated Ocala, between the years 1905 and 1965." The images, he said—of a hospital, of the Metropolitan Bank, of the wedding in Lincoln Heights—"reflect the determination, resourcefulness, and strength of many of our African American citizens who have come before us."[26]

Frank Gadson helped establish the Metropolitan Savings Bank, the only African American–owned bank in Florida when it opened in 1913.

The bank also owned the only knitting mill in the entire state, Metropolitan Hall, and the Metropolitan Theater. In 1915 George Mays, field director, gave a talk at the Lyric Theater in Miami, extolling the virtues of his alma mater, Booker T. Washington Institute, when he told the audience he "was glad he was born in the south . . . where the negro had plenty of good strong white friends who believe in him." The program included a showing of "garments made by the colored girls in the Ocala Knitting Mills," as "an inspiration to others."[27]

In 1917, the *Crisis*, the official publication of the NAACP, included a notice referring to African American soldiers about to enter World War I: "The thirty-five Negro draftees in Ocala, Florida were given a reception at the Metropolitan Theater, where addresses were delivered by the Mayor, postmaster, and prominent Negroes."[28] One of those draftees may well have been Dr. James Ponder, who attended school in Ocala before going off to Europe in 1917, where he served two years. He returned to Ocala after the war ended, set up a practice,

Timothy Howard, dressed as Santa Claus, poses with children at Paradise Park. To the left of Santa is civil rights leader Frank Pinkston, holding his child. Photo by Bruce Mozert. By permission of Bruce Mozert. Courtesy of Marion County Black Archives.

Founders of the Metropolitan Bank, the first African American–owned bank in Florida. *Left to right*: Dr. Reche Williams, Frank P. Gadson, George Giles, L. Wiley, St. George Richardson, David Walter Goodman. By permission of the State Archives of Florida.

and then later moved to St. Petersburg, where he became that city's first African American doctor.[29] Another might have been Levi Alexander Jr., who also went into the service in 1917; he was the son of the architect Levi Alexander, who built Mt. Zion, the oldest black church in Ocala.

According to historian David Jackson, Gadson and his partners in the Florida State Negro Business League were "inspired" by a visit Booker T. Washington made to Ocala at their invitation, when he spoke to crowds at a park. Robert Moton—principal of Tuskegee Institute in Alabama where the Tuskegee Airmen trained, and the man for whom their Moton Field training facility was named—was asked to sing by Washington, who commented that whites might be good at many things, but they couldn't surpass the black man at "making his own songs and singing them better than anybody else." In his autobiography Moton wrote about that moment when blacks and whites came together:

I do not think I ever had such a sensation as we experienced at Ocala, Florida, where he was greeted by probably twenty thousand people at the Fair Grounds. Just before Doctor Washington was presented to the audience by Judge W. S. Bullock of Ocala, he asked me to lead them in singing "In Bright Mansions Above"; and when we were all singing, the white people unconsciously [joined] in.[30]

As Joyce Hope Scott pointed out, the strength and cohesiveness that grew in this powerful African American community in Ocala and the surrounding areas resulted in the development of institutions like Howard Academy, later known as Howard High, and West Broadway, a street lined with black-owned businesses that became the center of black life in Marion County. Together these institutions formed a supportive culture similar to that described by Bernice Johnson Reagon in *The Songs Are Free*, a documentary history of music from slavery to the civil rights era. When asked by Bill Moyers how people sustained themselves in the Jim Crow era, she explained that they sustained themselves with what they created, an African American culture "that empowers you as a unit in the universe . . . and makes you know you are a child of the universe. When the culture is strong, you've got this consistency where black people can grow up in these places with this voice just resonating about our specialness in the universe."[31] This voice led to the creation of Paradise Park.

Howard Academy

In the 1950s a group of young women from Howard Academy gathered around a large arrow-shaped billboard emblazoned with the words: "See Silver Springs from Paradise Park for Colored People." They are dressed in their Sunday best, all white lace and tulle, standing in the grass beneath the sign, glancing at one another with shy smiles rather than at Bruce Mozert, the Silver Springs photographer. The image would be used on postcards and brochures or sent out to "colored" newspapers to draw in tourists. But the words "for colored people" on the sign behind them seem out of place here, because these young women do not have a trace of the shame that might have come with being treated as second class citizens. They are proud. They are students from Howard, one of the best schools in the state, and they can go to Paradise every day of the week.

Howard Academy for black students was opened in 1867 by the Freedman's Bureau. A former slave owner, James H. Howard, supplied the land, and the school was funded in part by northern patrons. One of the first teachers at Howard was H. W. Chandler, an African American lawyer, minister, and newspaper owner, who became Ocala's city clerk in 1876 and was elected a state senator in 1880. "Howard rose from the latter part of the 19th century, to become one of the most prestigious schools in the state. Through the years she helped to bring the light of knowledge, the love of learning, and the hope of historical change, and a dream of a better life for all who passed through her halls," noted Thelma Parker.[32]

As with the schools in most segregated communities, Howard Academy, despite being underfunded and neglected, was a bulwark in the community, as evidenced by the first stanza of the school song as remembered by LaRone Taylor Davis, class of 1960:

Dear Old Howard we are yearning, we will fight for you
Our loyal hearts are burning, we'll be ever true.
Howard, Howard bless her name, deeply graven on each heart.
We your loyal sons and daughters, pledge to do our part.[33]

Erma Rush graduated from Howard Academy in 1940, went off to college, then came back and taught at Howard for more than thirty years. She described how important an education was to her mother, who worked as a laundress at the segregated Marion Hotel and who would sit down with her children at the kitchen table late in the evening and help them with their schoolwork. "Everybody was striving to have their youngsters finish high school," Rush said of that period in the late 1930s when opportunities for African Americans were few. "They were striving because they didn't want to spend all of their lives working in fields and having nothing to do but maid's work."[34] Prior to the civil rights era, because of unequal funding for schools, the students at Howard had to use hand-me-down books from Ocala High, James Thorpe said. "When they got through using a book, they would give them to Howard Academy. That was our new books. You had teachers then who taught you something, and you couldn't go to school any kind of way."

The Gary sisters, June and Faye, do not remember the circumstances that led them to pose for the photograph beneath a Paradise Park billboard on Silver Springs Boulevard when they were teenagers. June remembers the pretty dresses they wore, and Faye remembers it was a Saturday morning. June guessed park manager Eddie Vereen may have arranged the shoot, since he knew their parents and they knew the girls would be in safe and wholesome company. Faye thought the shoot might have been organized by a teacher at Howard High School, since all of the girls in the photo were Howard students.

Given the trajectory of their lives—set in motion on a farm their grandfather William Primus Gary established long before the photo was made, indeed, long before they were born—it's understandable why posing for a photo decades ago would fade out of memory. Along with their

Left to right: Faye Gary, unknown, unknown, Lorraine Hollomon, and June Gary from Howard Academy pose next to a sign advertising Paradise Park. Photo by Bruce Mozert. By permission of Bruce Mozert. Courtesy of Cynthia Wilson-Graham.

grandparents, their father and mother, Homer and Ollie Colden Gary, instilled in them the principle that family, their farm, education, and achievement came first. Not only did June and Faye earn doctorates, their sisters Gladys and Ollie did as well, and each of them continues to distinguish themselves in their respective fields.

Dr. June Gary Hopps served as the dean of Boston College's Graduate School of Social Work before joining the faculty at the University of Georgia, where in 2013 she was named a Thomas M. "Jim" Parham Professor of Family and Children's Studies. While a student at Spelman College, she helped organize the Atlanta Student Movement and was arrested while participating in the first sit-ins and boycotts. Dr. Ollie Gary Christian was the chair of the Department of Social Sciences and Sociology at Xavier University before joining the faculty at Southern University, and Dr. Gladys Gary Vaughn headed up the American Association of Family and Consumer Science before entering her second career as special assistant to the assistant secretary for civil rights at the U.S. Department of Agriculture. Dr. Faye Gary taught at the University of Florida for over thirty years in both the College of Nursing and the College of Medicine before moving to Case Western University where she holds an endowed chair. This list doesn't begin to cover the honors, awards, books, firsts, and articles the four have compiled. Their brother, Homer Gary II, earned a bachelor's degree and continues to operate the family farm, along with the support of his four sisters.

"We grew up in south Ocala on Gary Farms," said June. "The farm was started by my grandfather and it was continued and built onto by my father. My grandfather moved from South Carolina to Florida as a very young person and he worked for a veterinarian and bought the first part of Gary Farms, which was a 160-acre tract in South Marion County. We've kept all of the Gary parcels and we inherited several hundred acres."[*]

Faye said that growing up on a working farm contributed to the mindset that led to their successes. Among the cattle and crops there were few distractions and cause and effect was clear: "If you wanted eggs you had to tend to the chickens," she said. "Your duties were to the farm and family." And to education.[†]

In an essay June wrote that was included in the anthology *Culturally Diverse Populations: Reflections from Pioneers in Education and Research*, she noted that her grandfather not only taught his grandchildren about the wonders of nature, but he also taught them to read before they even started school. When they went to school, he purchased new textbooks for them so they would not have to use those "handed down from White to Colored and all marked up with graffiti. . . . Of course, by the time a book reached my younger siblings, it was truly a hand-me-down, but the meaning, intent, and historical significance did not reek with the onerous whiff of discrimination and moral inferiority."[‡]

"My father and grandfather were about building petty wealth even in a segregated racist environment," June said, describing the legacy handed down in the family. "They fought segregation. They were not about integration," she said, and added that her father often employed white workers. "They were about desegregation and the purpose of desegregation was for a better allocation of economic resources which black people were entitled to but couldn't get. That was their fight."

Her mother got in on that fight as well. She was among the teachers who sought equal salaries for African American teachers along with Edward Davis and Harry T. Moore and for that she lost her job. "She was reassigned to another school later," said June. "She taught at Belleview-Santos and was the first African American teacher assigned to a predominately white school during the desegregation process."

"The emphasis at Howard High School was on academics," said June. "They used what I call the Greco-Roman model; you succeed academically and you succeed athletically. Because of segregation, talented 'colored people' couldn't teach anywhere, so they taught at Howard Academy, and later at Howard High and Howard Elementary. So those of us who came along in that period were the beneficiaries of very well-educated, very dedicated, and very strong teachers. My mother was one of them. She taught school for over forty years, and she was the principal of a small school, so we grew up in an environment where academic work was highly expected and recognized, and achievement was what you were supposed to do; it wasn't special," she said. "You were supposed to do well."[§]

Notes

[*] June Gary Hopps, interview by Lu Vickers, February 10, 2015.

[†] Faye Gary, interview by Lu Vickers, February 10, 2015.

[‡] June Hopps, Elaine Pinderhughes, and Tony B. Lowe, "A Journey Through the Prism of Race: An Evolution of Generational Consciousness," *Culturally Diverse Populations: Reflections from Pioneers in Education and Research*, edited by Diane De Anda, p. 231. New York: Routledge, 2013.

[§] June Gary Hopps, interview by Lu Vickers, February 10, 2015.

The teachers made up for what the county did not provide. Robert Williams, another former Howard student, told a reporter that E. A. Nelson, the art teacher at Howard, invited him in to use his art supplies. "I couldn't afford paint and brushes and things, but I knew I wanted to paint. It was in my blood. You could use anything. You were welcome in there anytime. He never turned me away."[35] This sort of commitment by teachers and principals was not unusual during the days of segregation; school officials often became a "family" of sorts, caring for the children financially, physically, and emotionally, right along with their parents.[36]

Loretta Pompey Jenkins, former principal of Fessenden Elementary School and President of the Marion County Branch of the NAACP, spoke about her experience at Howard. She graduated in 1961. "I guess you don't really look at it or kind of see how bad it was until you get older and look back. Going to Howard High was the most fun, the best years of my life growing up. It was totally segregated, but we had dynamic teachers. We had an integrated curriculum back then. . . . The English teacher would bring in newsworthy items about social studies and the history teacher worked with us on writing. We had the Thespian Society that did plays and went all over; we had athletics, the band. We had exposure to things they couldn't afford for the school. I remember the hand-me-down books, but the teachers maximized it, by helping . . . expose us to other things of life." She recalled that the teachers too had to struggle to get their degrees. "Because the University of Florida wouldn't let them in during that time, if they wanted a master's degree, they had to go to Columbia in New York or Indiana University."[37]

Dr. E. C. Mitchell Hampton, the first African American woman to become a doctor in Florida passed through Howard's halls, as did Dr. R. S. Hughes, who in 1925 established the American National Thrift Association Hospital on West Broadway to serve the African American community in Marion and other surrounding counties. Wayne Nielson, the postcard collector, came across a postcard depicting the hospital. "The people who received care in that hospital helped to shape Marion County to what it is today. But there is no mention of this hospital in *Ocali County*," he said, referring to an early book written about Ocala. "I want to learn more."[38] He needed to talk to Jennie Lee Laroche Harris, Dr. R. S. Hughes's niece and half-sister of Dr.

L. R. Hampton. While being interviewed about her missionary work in China she told the reporter, "Right now, you should learn about Dr. Hughes. We need to remember him and keep his memory alive. He was something like Dr. King. . . . His contribution was as much a contribution to whites as to blacks." She said she grew up at the hospital, a former boarding house, because her grandparents lived there. After the hospital was established, Hughes created the American National Thrift Association to provide health insurance to African Americans. The building was razed around 1956 when the City of Ocala widened Pine Avenue.[39]

Dr. Nathaniel Jones, Dr. Ernest Lamb, and civil rights leader Frank Pinkston Sr. also graduated from Howard. Over the years the academy has inducted outstanding graduates into its Hall of Fame, including Paradise Park's manager Eddie Vereen, journalist Thelma Parker, educators Edward and James Croskey, and Charles Bailey, the first African American from Florida to fly as a Tuskegee Airman in World War II. Charles was the last of the seven "Fighting Bailey Brothers" to serve in the armed forces—his brother Carl was one of the first African American jet pilots in the state, serving in Korea. Although Bailey was from Punta Gorda, there was no black high school in that county, so he

Paradise Park was a popular place for schools to bring children for educational field trips. Photo by Bruce Mozert. By permission of Bruce Mozert.

lived in Ocala and went to school at Howard, where he won a football scholarship to Bethune-Cookman. He was not alone. Howard was one of only two schools in the state that awarded high school diplomas to African Americans.[40]

Not only was Howard graduating the likes of Charles Bailey—the school also served as a center for civil rights. In 1937 members of the Florida State Teachers' Association met there to work on a plan for a lawsuit to "equalize salaries for white and black teachers." One of the teachers at that meeting was Harry T. Moore, a man who would become the first civil rights activist to die in Florida, along with his wife Harriette, when their house in Mims was bombed in 1951 as a result of his involvement in the infamous Groveland rape case.[41] "Harry Moore's daughter, Annie Rosalea, was a teacher [at Howard]," said Dr. Clarence Cotton. "She was a very good friend of my aunt. She married Dr. Hampton's son. When her family was killed at Mims, there was a shutdown in the black community. Your parents wouldn't let you out the door; the police advised us not to leave our homes. It wasn't the easiest thing growing up in that environment. Paradise Park was the outlet—everything else that was going on you had to accept—but Paradise Park was a social outlet."[42]

Part of being a social outlet meant being a place where children could learn to swim. In the 1950s Howard Academy was the spot where up to a hundred children would gather on summer days in the 1950s to board buses that would take them out to Paradise Park, where they eased into to the cold Silver River for swim lessons.[43] It is probably no accident that during this time the Paradise Park brochure included a photo of crowds of children swimming; the caption below the image made an emphatic statement: "Life Guards Will Protect The Children."

There are too many notable Howard alumni to list them all, but some of the standouts include Jesse McCrary, Howard's star quarterback and later Florida's first African American secretary of state; civil rights activist Reverend Frank Pinkston, and activist and attorney Dorsey Miller. Today the school is a community center and home to Head Start along with the Marion County Black History Archives, which maintains a collection of Paradise Park photos and memorabilia. Obviously Paradise Park played a role in the lives of Howard Academy students—it was their hangout. "When I was in high school on the football team," said Clarence Cotton, class of 1955, "we'd go to

Paradise Park to relax before games."[44] When Paradise Park celebrated its first anniversary, the Howard Academy band played, and the principal of the school led the program. When Susie Long Killins passed away in 1985 her obituary summed up the importance of each place in one sentence: "Mrs. Killins was a graduate of Howard Academy High School, class of 1951, and was crowned . . . 'Miss Paradise Park,' a beauty pageant which became a very prestigious event in this area."[45]

Paradise Park's lifeguards pose with Howard's class of 1955 on the white sand beach along the Silver River. Photo by Bruce Mozert. By permission of Bruce Mozert. Courtesy of Robert Thomas.

Ocala's Little Harlem

Paradise Park might have been the heart of Ocala's West Wide for the park's twenty years of existence, and Howard Academy its head, but come Saturday mornings, West Broadway Street was its soul. Eddie Vereen knew this and placed a big "See Paradise Park" sign on the side of one of the buildings lining the street. Ask an Ocala native of a certain age about West Broadway and you will get a list of businesses, small towns, superlatives. "It was like Times Square!" "It was like Las Vegas!" "It was like Harlem!" "It was Negro Heaven!"

Pinkney Woodbury, an activist and historian in Ocala, gathered a group of prominent African American leaders to compile *The Struggle to Survive: A Partial History of the Negroes of Marion County,* a book that would serve as a counterpoint to Ott and Chazal's *Ocali Country,* which left out most of the story of the West Side of Ocala. Woodbury himself was part of that struggle. In 1963, when he ran for a seat on Ocala's city council, the first African American to do so in the city in six decades, he got shot at three times but refused to drop out of the race. "They didn't want a black to break the ice at that time. I'd get calls almost every night from white folks. They always said 'this is the Klan.' They did it on account of hate. I always said, once I started something, I am going to finish. . . . They was going to have to kill me before I dropped out," he said in 1994, at the age of 81.[46]

Woodbury exemplified that strength in every aspect of his life, and even though he died in 2006, he is still remembered today for his tireless efforts on the part of his neighbors—particularly the children—who lived in Tucker Hill, a community on Ocala's West Side, where Howard Academy was first built.[47] Dolly Culpepper moved to this area as well when she was a teenager, to a neighborhood she called the "Green Quarter." She told a reporter that she and a group of friends

Susie Long Killins accepts her award and title of Miss Paradise Park in 1951. Photo by Bruce Mozert. By permission of Bruce Mozert. Courtesy of Cynthia Wilson-Graham.

formed a sort of club they called the Green Quarter Broads. The rules were simple: "A Green Quarter Broad was special. A Green Quarter Broad went to church and took her studies seriously, and any young man who wanted to go out with her had to ask permission of her parents and guarantee to have her home by curfew."[48]

The famous Reverend Mack King Carter grew up in and around Ocala and in 1973 married Patricia Thomas, the daughter of Silver Springs boat captain Nathaniel "School Boy" Thomas Jr. According to a reporter from the Broward County newspaper, he never forgot West Broadway:

> To hear Carter rhapsodize about Ocala in those sermons today, it seems he wants to return to the city—not modern-day Ocala so much as the Ocala of his youth. Or of his parents' youth, when all the businesses on West Broadway, from Magnolia to 16th avenues, were owned by black families. It was home to the best black hotel in the state and one of the few black banks in the South. The black preachers bought their suits, hats, and shoes from Crompton's Dry Goods Store, until its black owner, Gibbs Crompton, died in 1959.[49]

There were a skating rink, a meat market, shoe repair shops, a printing business and newspaper, and Joe Hall's Ice Cream Parlor, all owned by African Americans. West Broadway was also home to two black-owned pharmacies, Pinkston's and Mitchell's, as well as Black-owned businesses like L. C. Stevenson's pool hall. In addition to Crompton's Dry Goods, the area boasted several other stores including Long's Grocery and Market on Northwest 4th Street. Austin Long, ninety-two years old when interviewed for this book, opened his store two years before Paradise Park opened, selling snacks to students from Howard Academy. He said he never had the opportunity to visit Paradise Park because he was too busy managing his store.[50]

Howard graduate Effie Mitchell Hampton, the daughter of an ex-slave, became the first African American woman doctor in Florida in 1906 and set up a practice and pharmacy in a two-story building on West Broadway owned by R. S. Mitchell, her husband's grandfather. Her husband, Dr. Lee Royal Hampton, the first black dentist in Ocala, opened his practice in the same building but upstairs next to Hampton Hall, a popular night spot.[51] Dr. W. P. Wilson practiced in Ocala too, according to his nieces Johnnye Jacobs and Doris Jacobs-Smith. A brief clipping from the *Ocala Evening Star* mentioned one of his recent acquisitions: "Dr. W. P. Wilson, one of Ocala's most substantial colored citizens, has just received a buggy made especially for physicians by the big buggy factory at Greenfield, O., owned and operated entirely by negroes. The buggy is as fine as any in town."[52]

Dr. Clarence Cotton, who became a lifeguard at Paradise Park, said his father got his start in the dry cleaning business on Broadway. "Thank God my father—after being told by the man he was working for that he wouldn't give him a raise—left and started his own business. He got himself a cooling iron and went to Broadway and stood outside the pool room and the guys going in let him iron their pants. He started his business from that, and wound up having two dry cleaners, and I don't know how many houses he owned and rented out, plus an apartment building we ended up selling. For night clubs, you had the Night Owl, the Chicken Shack, Club Bali, the Brown Derby Club—one out on [highway] 27. I remember seeing Lionel Hampton and James Brown. Dinah Washington spent the evening before she performed at my aunt's house. The stars would come and visit the homes. The Club Bali was owned by Dr. Lamb, and he owned

two motels—one next to the club and one down on Broadway. When stars would come they would meet people and eat dinners with them. As far as Ocala was concerned, the West Side was the spot."[53] Some of the entertainers made their way to Paradise Park.

Henry Jones said one of his fondest moments was when B. B. King came to Ocala and stopped off at Paradise Park. "I took B. B. King out on the boat. . . . He appeared to be a thin man to me at that time. I was excited as I got to take him and his entourage out on a boat ride, but he didn't even give me a tip. Later, I saw him at Club Bali sitting on the edge of the stage. When they had big events, white people would come and sit in the balcony. Music is music; it's international and eliminates all craziness. The circuit was controlled," Jones said, referring to the "Chitlin' circuit," the group of mostly southern venues where African American musicians could play safely during the Jim Crow era. "Entertainers would come down to Tampa and end up in Miami," Jones said. "Sometimes they'd play down on Broadway, or upstairs in Hampton Hall. I saw Lionel Hampton in Hampton Hall; my mama kissed him on the cheek."[54]

On January 8, 1963, in his "Town Talk," a social column for African Americans, Julius Stafford wrote that James Brown would be making an appearance at the Club Bali that very night, and he included notes from their interview: "James is a qualified musician in his own right, playing drums and organs. He practices an hour and a half a day singing to keep his voice strong and unique as it is, but to the dismay of his band members, he calls a rehearsal every day in the week for at least four hours." This was about six months before Brown released his hit album *Live at the Apollo*.[55]

Arizona Vereen-Turner remembered that night. "I was out there when the Impressions were there, but I'll tell you who I never saw: James Brown. He was at Club Bali. My husband left me home to go get us a ride because we didn't have a car, and I saw him the next day."[56] Eddie Vereen is said to have had photos of all the stars that came through Paradise Park while in Ocala, but no one knows if the Godfather of Soul is among them.

On the weekends, before heading out to Paradise Park for a picnic and swim, a lot of people would flock to Broadway. "Saturdays, everyone would meet on Broadway, even families from the country drove in to visit and sell their buttermilk and produce," Sylvia Jones told the *Ocala Star Banner*. "There was a sense of community."[57]

Johnnye Jacobs and her sister, Doris Jacobs-Smith, the former curator of the Black Archives in Tallahassee, said they went to Broadway each weekend. "What was so amazing about it was that the different communities—Belleview, Shady Grove, our community, Watula, Martel, and Cotton Plant—had their certain area they parked on Broadway and off Broadway. We parked right on Broadway next to Pinkston's drugstore. The people from Shady Grove parked in the back near Mount Moriah church. The people from Belleview parked near Hampton Hall, and the parents would visit with different people. What all the children did is go to the movies. The Roxy was our theater downtown, but it burnt down when we were in grade school."[58] The Roxy served African Americans from 1937 until 1953 when it caught fire. It was owned by the Katiba Holding Company, which also owned the market next door. After the Roxy closed, said Doris, "We would walk all the way uptown to the Ritz, the predominantly white theater, right next to where Magnolia crossed Broadway. We went all the way upstairs to the balcony where the machines were running, and the whites sat on the ground floor."[59]

"Saturday was when all the blacks came to town shopping to get their groceries," said Virginia Ferguson. "You couldn't get through there for blacks and Indians," she said, referring to the Seminoles who lived at Silver Springs. "This was their recreation. They came to town from Lowell and Sparr, where I live, from Citra and Reddick, Anthony and Zuber, all those small towns. Everybody came out of the woodwork on Saturdays."[60]

Luresa Lake said when she got a new car, she knew to head over to Broadway to show it off. "I remember Broadway and the first car that I got. I don't remember the model but I remember the color; it was green, a new car. I had been riding in cars my entire life that were so 'piece of cars,' raggedy cars, and when I got the first car on my own, I rode up and down Broadway blowing my horn, and me and my kids were in the car, packed in and I was hollering out the window, 'Look at me! I have a new car!' That's the truth. I was so elated that I had a car I could ride in, that I didn't have to expect to break down. . . . People from Zuber, people from Belleview would all crowd up on Broadway on Friday and Saturday. You would meet people that you knew—the men would drink beer and the women would wander up the street or sit on the sidewalks and talk about what was going in each other's churches."

Lake was also Marion County's first African American deejay at WMOP, a radio station on Orange Avenue right off Broadway. "I was chosen to do a Sunday afternoon show and I would play all the records—Billy Eckstein, big shot bands like Count Basie. It was a black station, and black folk wanted to hear black musicians. I did that for a number of years," she said. "Everybody got used to listening to me," she said, slipping into her radio voice: '*Luresa Lake, your radio announcer coming to you this afternoon with music for your listening pleasure.*' That's the way I'd carry on because I was on the air. There were as many white listeners as black because people would call me and say 'I want you to play this' or 'I want you to play that.'"[61]

West Broadway definitely had a mix of the sacred and profane. Willie Eason, the "most influential sacred steel player, living or dead," used to play steel guitar on 20th Avenue and Broadway, his wife Jeannette told folklorist Robert Stone, author of *Sacred Steel: Inside an African American Steel Guitar Tradition*. Sacred steel is a form of African American Pentecostal gospel music that utilizes the lap and pedal steel guitar. It originated on the streets of Ocala when Willie Eason and his brother Troman arrived in town in the 1930s. Eason introduced the music in the House of God churches, originally founded in Tennessee in 1903 by Mary Magdalena Lewis Tate. She opened a church in

Ocala in 1914, which was headed up by Bishop Willie L. Nelson, who lived with his wife and children on West Broadway. Willie married Alyce, Nelson's daughter. His son Henry was another major steel guitar player who helped the church develop a following in Florida. Henry's mentor was Willie Eason.

Eason, who played with the Blind Boys of Alabama and Sister Rosetta Tharpe, "would go down to Buddy B's, and he'd hook up," his wife said. "That loudspeaker, when it went out, people out in the clubs and the bars, and even Dr. Hampton, he would open his windows. He was a dentist. He would open his windows to let the patients hear Willie playin'."

Stone, a musician and record producer, wrote that Henry Nelson, Eason's protégé (who also played football for the Wild Bulls of Howard Academy) was often nearby listening in. On that corner the crowd of appreciative listeners would try to get Eason to play secular songs like "Flat Foot Susie with the Floy Joy," and he would toss off a piece of the song, according to Mary Linzy, Nelson's sister. "That was a little joke for him," Linzy told Stone. "People were shoutin' on them corners when he played. But sometimes he would . . . do his little guitar with that, and that would just tickle them to death. But he don't go no further. . . . He's never, never, never played the blues—always songs he made, put together. And they were religious songs."[62]

When people finished listening to Willie Eason's steel guitar, they could head over to Miss Pearl's Restaurant on West Broadway. Miss Pearl Jackson opened the eatery in 1945 and served up dishes like smothered pork chops, barbecued chicken, and candied yams until 1997. She retired a month before her eighty-third birthday.[63] The restaurant was popular with whites as well. Ocala native Brenda Flynn said she grew up in Ocala "when it still had board sidewalks on Broadway. My dad used to both sell fish and buy fish from a fish market there, and at the end of the sidewalk, there used to be an elderly African-American man, blind, who used to sell boiled peanuts in a small brown sack—cost 15 cents. It was a big day out for me when Dad sold fish . . . 'cause I'd get the most delicious boiled peanuts! [Miss Pearl's] always operated the same way. Spoken menu only, a daily special that almost always included greens, and when she ran out of food, that was that. Period. Darned near everything cooked in a big stock pot and the best fried green tomatoes in the history of the South."[64]

3

African American History at Silver Springs

A River Runs through It

Robert, the negro pilot whom we pressed into service to guide us the last 25 miles up to Silver Springs has been steering boats on the river for fifteen years. He says that there are 999 bends in the Ocklawaha exactly. . . . He would point to one that looked just like the rest to all of us and say . . . just ahead of this one is an old cypress that was struck in '17 by a streak o' lightnin' and it's fixin' to fall. And he was always right.

BOYD FISHER, "FROM THE ATLANTIC TO THE GULF," 1927

It is painfully ironic that local African Americans had to go to Paradise Park to see Silver Springs, given their close ties to one of the largest artesian springs in the world as well as to the Silver and Ocklawaha rivers. When asked why his family lived so close to the water, Willie Marsh, one of the first African American boat drivers to work at both Silver Springs and Paradise Park, said, "I guess why we were so close was my great-grandmother's master owned Silver Springs. They didn't think it would amount to anything; it just dripped and dripped."[1]

As some of the first people to settle in Silver Springs, African Americans were part of the tourism industry in Marion County from its very beginnings, working on pole barges and steamboats that ferried freight and sightseers up the Silver River in the 1860s. Their descendants would become the Silver Springs boat captains, employees and patrons of Paradise Park. Tourists visiting Florida always found their way to the Ocklawaha River for a jaunt up to Silver Springs, largely

Tourists aboard the river steamboat *Okeehumkee* at Silver Springs, Florida. Hubbard Hart built the boat in 1873 for his Hart Line. He hired many African American men as captains and crew. By permission of the State Archives of Florida.

because of the accounts written by Harriet Beecher Stowe, Constance Fennimore Cooper, and the poet Sidney Lanier. By the mid-nineteenth century Hubbard Hart was operating a steamboat line that ran from Jacksonville to Silver Springs and down to Palatka and back, and his pilots were almost always African American men, a tradition that likely surprised travelers accustomed to white captains on rivers farther west, such as on the Mississippi. As historian Bradford Mitchell pointed out, the respect accorded to the African American captains on the Ocklawaha and Silver rivers during that period was extraordinary.[2]

Almost all these nineteenth-century and early twentieth-century accounts of travel to the springs describe African Americans in their various roles, from pilots to barge men, cooks and guides. In 1892 on a trip up the Ocklawaha, Charles Ledyard Norton described the "extreme crookedness of the stream, which could be likened to a series of capital S's." These twists and turns heightened his appreciation of the "the skill of the negro pilots, and the strength and endurance displayed by them in steering this complicated course."[3] Charles Dunning, a travel writer for *Lippincott Magazine*, described how he asked the African American pilot if the passengers would have to climb a tree if they met another boat on the narrow waterway. The pilot assured the writer he had the situation under control. "[The pilot] could not devote much time to conversation," noted Dunning, "for he was fully occupied with guiding the boat around corners so sharp as almost to be angles. He did it very skillfully; but he could not prevent the 'Okahumkee' from going full tilt into the shore every now and then."[4] These writers, mostly from the North, also frequently described the men's singing as if it was entertainment, unaware of the songs' cultural significance. Most of these early songs were born out of a cultural blend between the American slave communities and West African communities from which most slaves came, and far from being entertainment, they provided "sustenance to African Americans in the midst of intense racial oppression."[5]

The writer-tourists were often as fascinated by the beautiful songs the boatmen sang as by the scenery:

> Meanwhile, one of the group of negro deck-hands at the prow had begun to sing a plaintive melody, a sort of hymn; but breaking off suddenly, he rolled out the gayest tune imaginable, although this seemed to be a hymn too. One of the verses was, "If religion was a thing that money could buy / The rich would live and the poor would die." Then came a chorus that was taken up by all his companions. "Oh, I'm troubled; I'm troubled about my soul."[6]

In his 1875 book *Florida: Its Scenery, Climate, and History*, Sidney Lanier spends a couple of pages describing his astonishment at hearing Dick, the "Negro boatman," whistling a tune so beautifully that it "entitles him to rank as an orchestral instrument."[7] Although, like the others, Lanier romanticized the singing of the African American workers, the reality is that the work they performed on those river jaunts into what the brochures touted as a "mystical fairyland" was intense. The "torturous waterway" was lit by flaming pine knots burning in iron pots atop the "pilot house roofs." Although some black boatmen worked under the supervision of white pilots, navigating the sudden bends in the river, "standing forward, with poles to test the depth of the river, it was they who decided the channel through the watery wilderness."[8]

That hard work, along with the legacy of African American voices, led the Silver Springs owners to hire African American men exclusively as glass bottom boat captains when tourism arrived in full force in the 1920s. Leon Cheatom, who is white, started sweeping sidewalks at Silver Springs when he was thirteen and later drove the jungle cruise for Colonel Tooey, who released rhesus monkeys on the river to drum up excitement. Today Leon is known as "Mister Silver Springs" for his knowledge of the attraction. His father, father-in-law, uncles, and cousins all worked there. "It was a bad time in history," he said referring to the days of segregation that led to the development of Paradise Park. "But," he added hopefully, "it's behind us. Every glass bottom boat captain we had was black; there were no white men at all operating boats. They hired blacks because southern people loved to hear black men talk; he had that slang about him—he was sing-songing. The people loved it. Down here they used to play football with the fish; they'd make a bread ball and drop it into the spring and the black boat captain would get to talking and calling the game, and the catfish and bream would bump it around and they called it football."[9]

"Waiting for the Sunday Boat," by William Henry Jackson, around 1902. The photographer used a glass negative to capture the group of musicians at the boat dock at Silver Springs. Detroit Publishing Company Photograph Collection. Courtesy of the Library of Congress.

William Crowell began working at Silver Springs in the 1920s rowing glass bottom boats out over the spring. He was interviewed in 1984 as part of the Florida Folklife project. Photo by Nancy Nusz. By permission of the State Archives of Florida.

In a Florida Folklife interview, Willie Marsh and William Crowell, two of the earliest Silver Springs boat drivers who also worked at Paradise Park, commented on the music they heard along the river. "When they'd get off that that boat," Crowell said, "I could hear the old folks singing; boy, they could sing. Coming up the river I would hear voices in the air. . . . 'Here's a song I have,'" and in a quiet, gentle voice he sang, "Don't forget the teaching of your mother; don't forget the prayers you used to say, now I lay myself down to sleep, I pray the lord my soul to keep." The reporter clapped, then turned to Willie Marsh and said, "Now let's hear a song from the other side."

Marsh wasn't having it. He said, "I can't sing. They used to tape me and say 'You didn't know you sounded like that did you? Your next job, you should take up singing.' I couldn't sing. I really can't sing. I don't even sing in church. My brother can sing and whistle, but I just cannot sing. I've tried all my life. I cannot; God knows, I cannot sing."[10]

Crowell and Willie Marsh were both born in Silver Springs, as was Eddie Leroy Vereen, who would later become manager of Paradise Park. Marsh was born in 1905, Crowell in 1901. Both men remembered the steamboats; that era lasted until about the 1920s. Crowell recalled playing on the shores of the spring and later unloading freight from

TAKE ROWBOATS HERE TO SEE THE
BOILING SPRING AND LADIES' PARLOR
AND OTHER POINTS OF INTEREST THAT CAN NOT
BE SEEN FROM DECK OF STEAMERS.

A scene from Silver Springs at around 1900. A sign advertising a glass bottom rowboat is nailed to the tree. By permission of the State Archives of Florida.

the steamboats onto the trains that arrived at the headsprings. Marsh told a reporter he could "remember watching the big steamboats come up the river from Palatka. I used to ride them back and forth all the time."[11]

In the late 1860s Samuel Howse purchased the land around the main spring, built a house, and started an orange grove; he bequeathed these properties to his widow, and she entered into a deal with New York composer and betting house operator T. Brigham Bishop to build a two-hundred-room hotel. Howse's son Oliver recalled later that he ran a little business carrying passengers out over the spring in rowboats: "There were no glass bottoms in my rowboats, but tourists could get a very good view of the underwater scenes when the boats just drifted over the water." In the winter of 1894 Florida was hit with a deep freeze, and then both men lost their properties in a fire. Attorney H. L. Anderson bought up most of the land from Howse's widow and in 1895 began work to create a railway from Ocala to Silver Springs.[12]

Meanwhile an accident at the springs is said to have been the genesis of the glass bottom boat that would become Silver Springs' trademark. The story goes that a man dropped his wallet into the water and was unable to see where it landed because of the ripples. A house was being constructed near the spring, and someone got the idea to run over and get a pane of glass. When he placed it on the surface of the water, not only were they able to see the wallet—they also saw how beautiful the underwater world was.[13] According to *Ocali County*, a history of the area, "With the coming of tourists, a row boat was placed in use on the Springs. An added convenience was a wooden bucket, its solid bottom replaced by glass, which hung overboard to afford a clearer view of the sights below."[14]

A young man named Phillip Morrell is said to have invented the glass bottom boat after watching these people fumble around with their buckets. He went into business taking people out over the spring and rousted up so much business that H. L. Anderson filed a lawsuit to prevent him from using the docks at Silver Springs. Anderson then launched his own fleet of glass bottom boats.[15] Photographs from this

At the time he was interviewed for the Florida Folklife project in 1984, Silver Springs boat captain Willie Marsh had worked longer at the attraction than anyone else: forty-nine years. Photo by Nancy Nusz. By permission of the State Archives of Florida.

African American History at Silver Springs: A River Runs through It era feature African American men standing by their rowboats, apparently waiting for customers.

Hullum Jones is also credited with building a glass bottom boat. Willie Marsh said he remembered Jones. "In the paper, in the history of the spring they said some man named Morrell made the boat, but my recollection was Hullum Jones; he made it to fish in. He made a boat we could go fishing in. He was the best fisherman that I ever saw. He fished with sweet potatoes, fried bacon, bananas and fat meat, and he'd catch more fish than anybody else. I used to go down there to see if he left any sweet potatoes in the boat. Don't forget the bread too. Sweet potatoes, banana, bacon—that's what he'd put on his hook."[16]

A brief story in Leoneade Ramsey's *The Luffmans and Allied Families* geneaology confirms Marsh's memory that Jones was an avid fisherman. As a child Jones heard that Florida was a great place to hunt and fish, so he left his home in Illinois, took a boat down the Mississippi and another to Jacksonville, rode a train to Gainesville, then walked to Orange Lake, where he told folks later that he had found the "end of the rainbow," an enormous "fishing hole," and there he sat by day "pulling in the big ones." At night he would head over to Chambers Store and play his fiddle. His family remembered him as a "hunter, fisherman, trapper, cattle buyer, fiddler, would-be airplane inventor, best sugar cane grower and syrup maker in the area, cantaloupe and watermelon grower, good neighbor, easy going 'no-spanker' father, and devoted husband."[17]

Marsh said those early days with the first glass bottom boats were dangerous. "The steamboats would come in and just about run over the one or two glass bottom boats they had at the Spring at that time," he told a reporter. "The boy who operated the boats used to live at the Springs. There was a bell on the side of his house. When folks wanted to go out in the glass bottom boats, they'd ring that bell and he'd take them."[18]

In spite of Hart's steamboats, the arrival of the early glass bottom boats, and the glowing accounts of the wonders of Silver Springs, the area was still primitive and difficult to get to by land. George Carmichael and his son Ed came to Ocala in 1885 and went into the whiskey distillery business in downtown Ocala. Their success at selling whiskey produced in Ocala made it possible for Ed to buy up property around Silver Springs from Anderson. He soon launched the Silver Springs

Daylight Route, with the help of Frank Mathews, who came up with the idea and built a motor cruiser called the *City of Ocala*.[19] They soon added a second boat named the *Silver Springs* and began taking passengers from Silver Springs to Palatka over three rivers, the Silver, Ocklawaha, and St. Johns.

Willie Marsh recalled the Daylight Route as well. "I started working at the sawmill that used to be just up the river from the hotel. Our whole family worked out there. My dad used to be the head cook on the river boats. I'd ride along with him all the time." He started working at Silver Springs for Carmichael when he was eleven years old. "I'd mostly just help or get in the way. I started working for Mr. Carmichael and quit when Mr. Ray and Mr. Davidson sold out in 1965."[20]

He told the Florida Folklife reporter how he knew for certain he was eleven when he started at the springs. "I can remember one thing about my age. Mr. Carmichael was there; my daddy was the cook on the boat, a passenger boat from Palatka to Silver Springs; he cooked for him. . . . They'd get out there about 5 o'clock and they'd give them two meals a day—that was during the winter. Mr. Carmichael was going to Oklahoma to speak to his second wife. . . . I always wanted to drive. They had chauffeurs back then, so I said, 'Mr. Carmichael, let me drive you; let me be your chauffeur.'

"'Oh no,' he said, 'I'll let you drive when you get to your teens.'"

"And I said, 'Well, I'm eleventeen.' So evidently I was eleven—I just put teen on it. I was just down there to get something to eat because my dad was the cook. In order to get something, I had to be on the job."[21]

William Crowell began working at Silver Springs in 1918 or so, initially working on the grounds. "We would work at hauling dirt until we got two or three customers, then we would stop that and take the customers on the river in the glass bottom row boats." He said it was nearly impossible to paddle back up the river after a tour. "We used to row down the river, and they would pull us back up the stream with an outboard."[22] Later, he recalled, "We used to paddle the boats out into the Spring for $2 a day in wages that Mr. Carmichael would pay us. Of course, that included all you could eat in the hotel kitchen," he said, referring to the Brown House that replaced the one T. Brigham Bishop owned before it burned down.[23]

Eddie Vereen also used to take trips on Ed Carmichael's Daylight

Route, according to his nephew Henry Jones. "When he was a boy there was a boat that would come up from Palatka on the St. Johns River," he said. "It was a double decker tourist boat out of Palatka. It would dock at Silver Springs. You couldn't have an open paddle; the trees and bushes would hit it. The paddle had to be protected. Uncle Ed used to catch small alligators and sell them to the tourists. The Vereens are from Silver Springs," he added, "on the north side of the highway. The church they attended is still there with the same benches: Mount Nebo."[24]

There might have been enough tourists for young Eddie Vereen's baby alligator sales, but there weren't enough for Ed Carmichael. He lamented the lack of tourists in the booklet he created to promote the springs, citing an interview with George Phillips, an agent with the Seaboard Air Line Railway:

> As it is, here in Florida, Silver Springs is very little known and there has never been any special effort made by any one to put before the tourists who visit Florida the wonderful beauty of these springs, and the very unusual and extraordinary sights that meet one on every hand when one takes a trip in a glass-bottom boat down the Silver River from Silver Springs to the entrance of the Ocklawaha.[25]

Carmichael's guide also features the "Legend of Osceola," a story Ray and Davidson would continue to use as a tourist lure. The man in the photo accompanying the story is definitely not Osceola; he is wearing a feathered headdress unlike what the Seminoles wore. However the legend relates that Osceola, who lived in Fort King, near Ocala, simply drove "his hunting knife through the midst of the document, left it, and walking from the council room, mounted his horse and rode away."[26]

He also included in full a version of "The Bridal Chamber of Silver Springs," by Maley Bainbridge Crist, a legend that featured Aunt Silla, a former slave who became somewhat of a tourist attraction at the springs for her role in a love story gone wrong. Aunt Silla herself would tell the story of the two ill-fated lovers, the rich Clare Douglas and the poor Bernice Mayo, who, unable to be together in life, would be joined in death. In the story Aunt Silla would facilitate their union by rowing Bernice out to what was previously known as Boiling Springs and dumping Bernice overboard. The story is similar to "The

Legend of Winona," which was apparently used at Silver Springs at some point. It featured a Native American maiden and a young warrior from another tribe. Former Silver Springs marketing director Steve Specht told a reporter that "the Bridal Chamber is really like a variation. Somebody embellished the Winona legend. Those were stories boat captains used years ago to help entertain guests on the glass bottom boat rides."[27]

However, Aunt Silla was a real person with connections to Paradise Park. According to Joyce Hope Scott, whose children claim kinship to Aunt Silla through their father, her name was Priscilla Scott, variously shortened to "Scilla," "Silla," "Lucilda," "Cilla," and even "Silly."[28] In 1874 Rufus Morgan, a North Carolina photographer and adventurer, published a stereograph image he made of "Aunt Cilla's cabin" at the springs with her standing before it alongside a young man. William Crowell and Willie Marsh, who were cousins, claimed Aunt Silla as kin. Marsh told a reporter that he had issues recounting that story for the tourists at Silver Springs and Paradise Park. "All that big story they

Aunt Silla was an ancestor of some of the boat captains at Silver Springs. She is seen standing beside the *Astatula* at the Silver Springs dock in the late nineteenth century. She made a living telling the tale of the "Bridal Chamber." By permission of the State Archives of Florida.

told about Aunt Silla, that bridal chamber and all that stuff. They [my grandmother and mother] declared they didn't know anything about that story. It's about the two lovers who were in love; she dumped [Bernice] out there in that bridal chamber because they wouldn't let them get married. They were heartbroke. That's the only thing I didn't like about it, because I didn't figure anybody would treat people like that. It was a great story, but I always put myself out there by saying 'It's said to be,' 'It's supposed to be.'"[29]

Eddie Vereen's niece Sylvia Jones shared his misgivings. "My grandmother, Mary Vereen Jones, whom I called Mama, and Uncle Eddie were born and raised in Silver Springs, and they played in the Silver River. I went to the homestead in the forest with Mama and Uncle Eddie. Mama would go down the river on the jungle cruise, and show me certain spots where they played as children. Aunt Silla was her aunt, and Mama was offended when they talked about lovers' leap and how the slave rowed the lovers out because they wanted to die together. Mama said her Aunt Silla was not an ignorant person. She might have been a slave, but she had plenty of sense and she never would have done that."[30]

"I got Aunt Silla's picture," Crowell told the Folklife interviewer, "and the owners were putting their hands on Aunt Silla. That was way back then. She died."[31] The photograph is in the Florida State Archives as well, and indeed Aunt Silla is standing next to a train, and each of the two men is touching her. In 2001 Aunt Silla was recognized in the Marion County Museum of History. "There was a time when the Silver Springs boat guides told all kinds of interesting local tales to the passengers," said the director, Bettie DeBary, referring to Aunt Silla and to the African American boat captains. "They lost a lot of that heritage when they no longer used the black native guides."[32]

4

The Ray and Davidson Era

It's not the same place I knew in 1912, but it is a wonderful place.
The grizzled boatmen who repeated the fantasies of the Indian maiden
who flung herself into the water rather than lose her love, and whose
face can be seen on some days when the light is right . . . painted the
scenery with tints of illusion . . . those old boatmen's soft-voiced tales
were the meat and potatoes of my early knowledge of the springs
when the feathered oars took us downstream and his soft voice spun
a wondrous tale.

HARDY CROOM, "MAN HAS SEEN CHANGES IN SILVER SPRINGS"

In 1909 after Ed Carmichael bought the eighty acres surrounding the
headwaters of Silver Springs, he set out to attract tourists by adding canopies to the glass bottom boats and installing nicer benches.
Drivable roads were finally constructed to the springs and the silent
film *The Seven Swans* was made on location there, giving Silver Springs
national attention; however, Carmichael was unable to draw the numbers of people he dreamed of attracting. That did not stop others from
eyeing the property for themselves. In fact, according to Richard Martin, two men were "intrigued and challenged" by the unrealized potential of Silver Springs as a tourist attraction. Colonel William M.
"Shorty" Davidson was a colorful man who favored cowboy hats and
bolo ties; he owned and operated Union Station, a popular café he
opened during World War I. Ray was the son of a turpentine man and
sawmill owner and was himself a successful contractor.[1]

Bill Ray told Tim Hollis, author of *Glass Bottom Boats* and *Mermaid
Tails* and many other books on tourism, that his father had visited
Silver Springs when it was owned by Carmichael. "When my dad was

Silver Springs employed only African American men to captain the glass bottom boats during the early years. By permission of Lu Vickers.

a young man, he would visit Silver Springs and he'd say, 'If people just knew about this place, they'd want to come and see it.' So when he was older he wanted to lease the property—about 80 acres around the head of the spring. The owner, Mr. Carmichael had several different business ventures, including a boat ride. Well, every time Dad thought he had a deal with Mr. Carmichael, the price would change. So finally after one of their meetings, Dad left and parked his car where no one could see it, and watched."[2]

Shorty Davidson showed up, and Ray realized what was happening: Carmichael was manipulating the two of them. Ray had a talk with Davidson, they decided to join forces, and in 1924 they formed the company Ray and Davidson. One of the first things they did was equip the glass bottom boats with gas-powered motors. Crowell and Marsh found themselves working harder than ever. "Things began to pick up after Mr. Ray and Mr. Davidson bought the property," Crowell said in

1983. "[They] replaced the paddles with gasoline engines. That meant we had to yell above the engines to tell the passengers what they were looking at. They had no loudspeakers then."[3]

Ray and Davidson each brought different qualities to the venture; Ray was a businessman and Davidson was the flamboyant promoter. When a Paramount newsreel team visited Ocala in the early 1920s, Davidson jumped into a pool of water in his swimsuit and was filmed eating a banana underwater. In 1929 a short film featuring Johnny Weissmuller was shot at the springs, and as Davidson said, this really put the place "on the movie map of the world." By 1931 nearly every studio in the country had dispatched film crews to Silver Springs, and before long Tarzan arrived. Johnny Weissmuller made six Tarzan movies at Silver Springs, and local African American men were hired as extras for some safari scenes.[4]

The first inkling of Paradise Park came just three years after Ray and Davidson took over, but it wasn't the Paradise Park that African Americans would visit. In fact, if the brochures were any indication, this Paradise Park was decidedly anti–African American. If Ray and Davidson had had their way, no one would have visited this version of Paradise Park. In 1927 a man named M. R. Porter purchased around 750 acres on the south side of the river and, by 1928, announced he would develop a park that would rival Silver Springs with features such as the "Pool of Salome," the "Primrose Path," and the "Elysian Island." He would call it Silver Springs Paradise. Originally known as South Beach, the area was on the southern side of the Silver River, just a short boat ride from the head of the springs.[5] Undaunted, Ray and Davidson began a legal battle that would last five years and would involve some shady activity, like plowing up the road that led to the attraction. They finally wore Porter down, setting off a series of further twists and turns. He sold the property to a group of investors, directed by E. H. Elarbee, and they formed the Silver Springs Paradise Company and began operating glass bottom boats on the river, spurring Ray and Davidson to file a suit claiming they owned the "bed of the river," in an attempt to prevent the boats from entering the head of the springs.

A judge ruled in favor of Davidson and Ray, but Elarbee and company appealed. While the battle went on in court, the Silver Springs Paradise Company continued operating boats on the river. In 1931 a

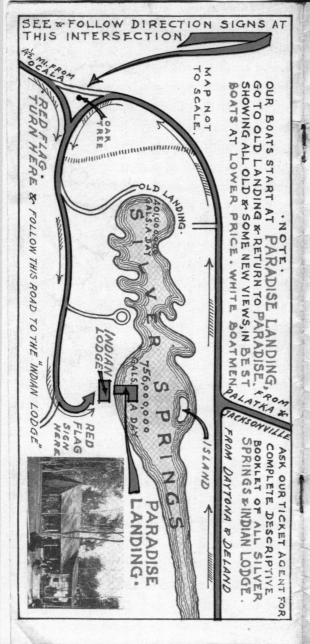

This is a brochure from the Silver Springs Paradise Park Company that was in direct competition with Silver Springs in the 1930s. The company advertised its "white boatmen" in contrast to Silver Springs, who at that time only employed African American boat captains. By permission of Cynthia Wilson-Graham.

federal court reversed the original decision, saying that Elarbee had a right not only to use the river but also to use the name Silver Springs.[6] The group advertised this ruling in their brochure, stating, "The courts ruled that the waters of Silver Springs belonged equally to all. We now show ALL SILVER SPRINGS FROM PARADISE PARK LANDING." Clearly, they didn't mean it really belonged equally to all, a fact underscored by this racist pronouncement: "OUR BOAT GUIDES ARE ALL INTELLIGENT WHITE MEN," a point they emphasized prominently on the front and back covers of the brochure: "WHITE BOATMEN."[7] The message was clear. Ray and Davidson employed only African American men to pilot their boats.

Ray and Davidson refused to accept the decision and went to the United States Supreme Court but were turned away. Finally, in 1931 Scott Appleby bought the property and by 1935, seemingly worn out by the legal issues, sold it to Ray and Davidson.[8]

Meanwhile, back at the main spring, Davidson and Ray built bathhouses and beautified the landscape by planting palms, some of which were the famous horseshoe palms the attraction would feature prominently in publicity photos and postcards. Over the next couple of decades they worked hard to make Silver Springs known the world over. "For the first ten years they were in business, Dad got his gasoline and cigarettes out of the profits," Bill Ray told Hollis, "and Shorty got his gasoline and pipe tobacco, and that was all they took out of the money. Every other penny they got was put back into building up the business and the advertising. They spent a huge amount of the income on the advertising." Davidson promoted the springs by sending out fleets of trucks fitted with dioramas of the glass bottom boats drifting over Silver Springs and by dotting the landscape with billboards directing tourists to Silver Springs.[9]

One of those tourists was President Calvin Coolidge. When he visited Silver Springs in 1928, William Crowell took him and his entourage down the river. Horace Smith, who was head of Ocala's Chamber of Commerce at that time, recalled the visit in an interview in 1970. "[The President] sat through the whole boat trip without saying a word, not even when they gave him bread to feed the fish. He put his hand out on top of the water and fed the fish, but the expression on his face never changed. . . . The poor guide was really trying to point out the interesting sights along the river but his was a difficult job, not being able to tell if the president was enjoying his lecture or not."[10] Apparently Crowell made an impression, because as a reporter noted in 1963, "Word is, however, that Silent Cal broke his well-known reticence long enough to express his delight with the famous boat ride." Over the forty-two years he worked at Silver Springs and Paradise Park, Crowell took out many famous people, from Johnny Weissmuller to presidential candidate Adlai Stevenson, who reportedly confided to Crowell that his election would be assured if all the fish in Silver Springs could cast a vote.[11]

However, despite having lived less than a mile from the springs his entire life, and despite having worn out fifteen boats in thirty-five years, Crowell himself was not allowed to visit the springs, or take his family for a glass bottom boat ride unless he went to Paradise Park and boarded the boat there. When he was at work, he would have to use the "Colored" bathroom and drink out of the "Colored" water fountain. It must have been a shock to him when, in 1963, he flew to New York to appear on Arlene Francis's show *What's My Line?* for her birthday. At that time he piloted the boat named *Arlene Francis* and had worked at Silver Springs for thirty-six years and logged more than 1 million miles on the river. A couple of years before he was chosen to go to New York, he had taken Francis out on his boat when she filmed her show at Silver Springs. "They sent me to New York to present her roses," he said later. "I went on the train, had the reservations for 2–3 weeks. I was so nervous; the lights were so bright, I couldn't stand it." She didn't recognize him, and he won $160. "I got everything they had. I was on a jet airplane coming back. I was so scared . . . I missed my dinner."[12]

The glass bottom boats piloted by Crowell and other African American boatmen were featured on pennants, in snow globes, on postcards, on spoons, on key chains; in short, on practically every piece of merchandise and advertising that came out of Silver Springs. Many of the brochures and postcards from this period feature a close-up of the glass bottom boat filled with hat-wearing white tourists and with a white-suited African American captain at the helm.

Clifford "Dizzy" Thomas managed the Silver Springs outdoor advertising. He would head north on Highway 441 and drive all the way to Nashville, Tennessee, then south to New Orleans, or north to Cincinnati and Washington, D.C., plastering the roadside with billboards the

Silver Springs only hired African American boat captains. Here a brochure has as its center of focus one of the captains with a group of white tourists. By permission of Lu Vickers.

whole way. He was responsible for hauling a Silver Springs diorama—including model glass bottom boats—all the way to Austin, Texas, on his first trip in 1931.[13] In the mid-1940s George Bolton became director of public relations at Silver Springs and he began hauling the diorama around, city to city. "We had the best exhibit," he told a reporter in 1983. "It was a moving replica model of the Springs, complete with moving glass bottom boats, monkeys that scampered about in the trees, fish that swam in the water and Ross Allen holding a squirming snake."[14]

Nathaniel "Pepper" Lewis captained a boat at Silver Springs through the 1960s. "When people got on the boat, we'd do our spiel," he said. "We'd tell them about the different springs; we had about seven or eight, and we'd go all the way down the river almost to Paradise Park, and we'd turn around and go back up to Silver Springs. There were a lot of fish in the river at the time. In the Catfish Hotel there were catfish so large, it was a shame but we'd show them how the catfish and the bream would play football together. We'd take a ball of bread and roll it up and drop it into the spring and the catfish always won. And we'd go up to the head spring where the water came into the river, and we'd tell them about that one. It was really nice."[15]

Henry Jones recalled that despite the rule against fishing on the river near the springs, Bill "Blue" Ray, Silver Springs publicity manager, did his own version of angling on the river, and so did the captains. "He could outswim Esther Williams, and he would catch those soft shell turtles and carry them out the water. You couldn't fish at Paradise Park; we'd fish with our hands. You'd reach out the window with some bread cupped in your hand next to the boat and the fish would come up—and you'd catch five or six nice little bream." He laughed. "I didn't want to tell you that back there where the guys park the boats—they had a hook and they'd drop it off down by the steering wheel. They could fish right through the hole. They were off duty and they'd catch a mess to take home."[16]

Some people wanted to do more than fish. In his interview with the Florida Folklife program in 1984, Willie Marsh told a couple of funny stories about the white tourists he took out up at Silver Springs. "I went down the river with a man and his wife once. She seemed to be very young. And she intimated—I don't know what she said to me now, I really don't, but whatever it was, she intimated to me that she wanted me to push him overboard and let him drown. She made me so mad. She saw that I wasn't going for it and switched the conversation. I got so mad."

Then there were the white folks' teeth. "When that vegetation would clear off out there during some months in the summer, you could see as many false teeth sets down there as you wanted. That's where they'd lean over to feed the fish and those things would drop out and they wouldn't mention it. I saw a man drop his teeth out there. I was about half mad and he was 'bout to say something and his teeth fell in the water, and he turned around quick; he didn't want me to see him. But I sent somebody to pick them out. Because I knew where they were."

Marsh retired in 1965. When the Folklife reporter asked him in 1984 if Silver Springs had given him a lifelong pass for his forty-nine years as a captain, he told her, "They offered me one, an annual pass but they never sent it. Never did."[17] However, in 2008, after he had passed away, the city of Ocala did recognize Marsh and his wife Weida S. Marsh, the first black principal at Madison Street Elementary School, by naming a street W. S. Marsh Avenue. Bill Ray said Willie Marsh stood for the best as far as boat captains went; he was "able to get along with and entertain people." Ray himself remembered going along on boat rides with Marsh when he was a child. At the road-naming ceremony, officials noted that Marsh had been the admiral of the boat fleets and still found time during World War II to teach welding classes. More than forty years after his retirement, he was publicly recognized at this 2008 ceremony for having worked longer at Silver Springs than any other employee.[18]

5

African Americans in Florida's Tourist Industry

Skipper Lockett knows how many clouds float daily over Rainbow Springs. He knows each tree bending beautifully over the translucent waters. . . . All that Rainbow Springs means to him—its music, its beauty, its history, he has gathered in a haunting chant for his passengers.

LORNA CARROLL, "THE BARD OF RAINBOW SPRINGS"

In the Jim Crow era in Florida, hiring African Americans as guides to entertain tourists as Silver Springs did was not an anomaly; it was standard practice. According to the Florida Memory project, "The amenities and services offered at Florida roadside attractions, from guided tours and local 'storytellers' to porters, drivers, and housecleaners, were often made available through the labor of African-Americans."[1] That is obviously an understatement, given the reality that Florida's economy was transformed by the largely African American workforce employed to build Henry Flagler's Florida East Coast Railroad.

Not only did Flagler employ African American labor along with Bahamian and Caribbean workers to build the railroad; he also employed them to build hotels such as the Hotel Ponce de Leon in St. Augustine, the Royal Poinciana Hotel in Palm Beach, and the Colonial, in what would soon be known as Miami. Communities such as the Styx in Palm Beach and Colored Town (later known as Overtown) in Miami sprang up to house workers, many of whom then stayed on to drive pedicabs and carriages or work as maids, butlers, and gardeners.

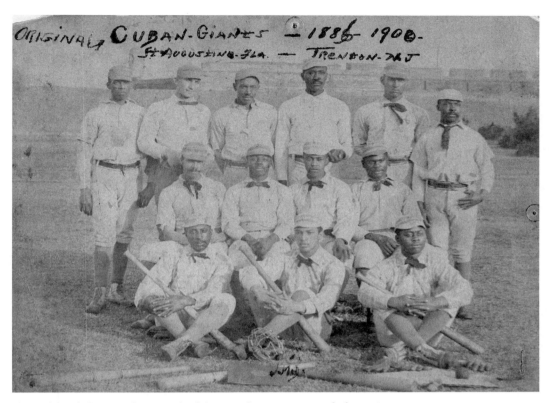

This is the only known photograph of the proud 1885–86 team of African American ballplayers known as the Original Cuban Giants. Not only were they the first professional (that is, salaried) all-black ball club, but they were the first to play against white Major League teams before the color barrier was dropped. When they went to play ball in Havana, Cuba, they were also the first professional ball club, black or white, to travel outside the United States to spread the baseball gospel. Catcher Art Thomas was offered but turned down a contract to play with Philadelphia in the Major Leagues. Player Milton Dabney was the original owner of this photo.

Left to right: (*standing*) Andrew Randolph, 1st base; Harry Johnson, 2nd base; Ben Holmes; Shep Trusty, pitcher; Art Thomas, catcher; and G. Day; (*center row*) Billy Whyte, Ben Boyd, George Parego, and Clarence Williams; (*front row*) G. Shadney, Milton Dabney, and S. Epps. Caption detail provided by Frank Ciresi and Carol McMains. By permission of the National Pastime Museum.

Some "Negro League" baseball teams, like New York's Cuban Giants, Chicago's American Giants, and New York's Lincoln Giants, used Flagler's hotels as a base for their tours of the southern states, sometimes working as waiters and bellhops and playing exhibition games under the names of Flagler's hotels for the guests. The Ponce de Leon Giants team was made up of members of the Cuban Giants' team, and the Breakers Hotel fielded players from the Lincoln Giants. According to Frank Ciresi and Carol McMains, the Cuban Giants "were the most historically important and significant black ball club of the 19th century . . . [the] very first black ball club whose players were regularly paid for plying their trade on the baseball diamond."[2] The hotel received free publicity, and the players had a safe place to stay in an era when Jim Crow laws made it difficult to travel. Hotel guests got to see "fast balls blown past batters by Smoky Joe Williams, regarded by many as a better pitcher than the legendary Satchell Paige; homers belted by the likes of Louis Santop and Oscar Charleston; ground balls fielded by the greatest of the black shortstops, John Henry Lloyd, a Floridian who played for the Breakers."[3]

Often some of the bellhops, butlers, and maids employed by these hotels would perform in cakewalk contests for the hotel guests. The cakewalk is an exaggerated dance that is said to have originated in Florida, when slaves mimicked dances performed by the Seminoles; it then spread across the South.[4] The dance was quickly transformed as a former slave explained: "Us slaves watched the white folks' parties where the guests danced a minuet and then paraded in a grand march, with the ladies and gentlemen going different ways and then meeting again, arm in arm, and marching down the center together. Then we'd do it too, but we used to mock 'em every step. Sometimes the white folks noticed it, but they seemed to like it; I guess they thought we couldn't dance any better."[5] By the 1900s the *New York Times* observed that the "moonlight cakewalks are among the most characteristic and picturesque of the Palm Beach functions." A thousand hotel guests dressed to the nines would take their place on the lawn beneath the "tall cocoanut palms hung with colored lights" to cheer the butlers and maids as they promenaded to win the cake and cash, oblivious to the double meaning of the dance.[6]

While many of Flagler's hotel employees lived in housing he provided, or in communities they created, many African American workers were transient, arriving in Florida with their white employers. A short tongue-in-cheek clip in the *Evening Independent* in 1929 noted that a "colored maid stated this morning that there were many negro tourists in the city at present." The article goes on to explain:

These "tourists" amuse themselves with light and congenial employment like playing nurse to white children while their men friends are to be seen at the wheels of expensive motor cars. They uniformly seem to be having a better time than any of the white winter visitors who employ them and they enjoy the society of acquaintances made in the negro section.[7]

The African American workers were often looked on not just to drive the tourists around but to entertain them with the colorful histories—some true and some not—of the cities and towns where they worked. As the *New York Times* pointed out: "For short jaunts round the cities there is the horse-drawn surrey driven by a Negro familiar with folk tales of the country."[8] Of course the drivers' own powerful stories went unheard for the most part. Alice Moore's father, Haley Mickens, owned a concession for the bicycle-powered rickshaws that served patrons of E. R. Bradley's Beach Club casino in Palm Beach. Although today the "Palm Beach chariots" are seen as demeaning, Moore told a reporter, "It was a way of life. The people they pulled, they were very nice. Some of them would tip heavily." Her father helped establish Payne Chapel A.M.E. Church—Palm Beach's first African American church—and her mother, Dr. Alice Mickens, participated in the civil rights battle in West Palm alongside her husband, hosting such luminaries as 1950 Nobel Peace Prize laureate Ralph Bunche, Mary McLeod Bethune, and A. Philip Randolph.[9] Today their home is listed on the National Register of Historic Places as one of the oldest continuously black-owned residences in West Palm Beach.[10]

The Breakers Hotel in Palm Beach, like other hotels built by Henry Flagler, employed African American men to drive their wicker "wheel chairs" for wealthy tourists. By permission of Lu Vickers.

A group stands by the bath house at Butler Beach on Anastasia Island in St. Augustine. According to the Florida Memory project, Butler Beach was "the only beach African Americans were allowed to use between Jacksonville and Daytona Beach. Developed by Frank B. Butler, who owned a casino, inn and other businesses, as well as building a subdivision of black owned homes." By permission of the State Archives of Florida.

African American workers such as Jim Doles helped construct Cypress Gardens, and then, once the gardens were established, the attraction employed only black waiters in its Palm Terrace Restaurant. They weren't allowed to visit the attraction, however, except on one day a year when the gardens were opened for "Negro Day," a strange feature of Jim Crow life.[11]

Long before tourists began arriving in Florida, St. Augustine was home to Fort Mose, the country's first free black settlement. Spanish Florida, as scholar Henry Louis Gates Jr. wrote, was "the African-American slaves' first Promised Land. At least since 1687, if slaves made it down to Florida, and professed belief in 'the True Faith'—Roman Catholicism—they were declared to be free."[12] And for a while they lived in Fort Mose, a city of their making. America's oldest city is also home to Lincolnville, a black neighborhood established by freed slaves in 1866 that later became home to Frank Butler. Butler was an African American entrepreneur who opened the Palace Market in 1914 and parlayed his success into real estate development. He purchased beachfront property on Anastasia Island in 1927 and, despite white opposition, established Butler Beach at a time when there were no beaches available for African Americans from Daytona north to Jacksonville. The beach was so successful that by the late 1930s Butler added a casino and a hotel.[13] In 2000 Frank Butler was recognized as a Great Floridian.

Despite Butler's success in St. Augustine, the first African American to be immortalized in a monument in the city was Major Argrett, a carriage driver who represented an important aspect of St. Augustine's 450 years of black history.[14] The city depended on the St. Augustine Transfer Company, a carriage service begun by the Colee family in 1877 to cater to the white tourists who arrived in droves on the Florida East Coast Railroad during the winter. In 1946 *Ebony* magazine devoted an entire article to the fifty or so "top-hatted colored drivers and their elegant surreys," like Henry James and Alec Nateels, who added ambience to the "old world atmosphere" by telling tall tales to gullible tourists, like the one about how the lighthouse originally had horizontal black and white stripes but then a violent storm whirled it around "causing a barber pole effect."

The Chamber of Commerce prided itself on the drivers "as a romantic remnant of old times," noting that "many people do not think of

African American carriage drivers were considered "landmarks" in St. Augustine. They told folktales as they drove tourists around America's oldest city. By permission of Lu Vickers.

St. Augustine without some thought of the hacks and colored drivers. . . . Individually they are some of the best salesmen for the community. . . . It would be a great loss if they were ever to discontinue their service."[15] Major Argrett, who drove carriages from 1910 until shortly before his death at ninety-six in 1984, caught the attention of a *National Geographic* editor who featured him in a story on the 400th anniversary of the town's existence. According to David Nolan, an author from St. Augustine, as the two men drove around town Argrett told the editor, "Don't you believe everything I say. You just believe about half what I say, then you safe." He paused and added, "I talk long enough, there bound to be some truth in it." Nolan wrote that "some of St. Augustine's greatest folklore—then and now—has come from the mouths of carriage drivers."[16]

At Wakulla Springs in North Florida, African American men began rowing tourists out over the spring the late nineteenth century. In 1890 author Hezekiah Butterworth visited Wakulla Springs and wrote later how he hired a "negro boatman" to take him out. "Look down," the boatman said when they got over the springhead; then he dropped a nail into the water, which was so clear that Butterworth thought he was suspended in air until he saw the "bubbles [arise] like gems of all hues."[17] In 1931 descendants of some of those original boatmen began operating the glass bottom boats at Wakulla, even as they and their families were prevented from enjoying the springs outside of work because of segregation. Luke Smith rowed his boat and sang of the underwater plant life, and boatman Tom Gavin sang of the vultures that sat up in the cypress trees: "Some people refer to 'em as a country airplane. . . . In some of those other places, they refer to 'em as the undertaker's helper." He also created the legend of Henry the Pole Vaulting Fish—which became a selling point for Wakulla—after watching a bass rub its body against a log lying at the bottom of the spring. His singing chant to call up the fish to perform was passed down to his nephew Don Gavin and to other boatmen.[18] When a *New York Times* reporter visited Wakulla in 1996, he took a glass bottom boat tour piloted by A. J. Rainey, with a group of white American tourists and "a couple of Germans thrown in for variety." As the boat drifted past a moccasin, Rainey got to work with his spiel: "Now I know the ladies love snakes. Snakes is a lady's best friend. But don't worry, be happy—we're going to find a snake for every lady on this boat, just

Manning "Skipper" Lockett became a boat captain at Rainbow Springs in 1934. He was famous for his chant, which he often performed at the Florida Folk Festival in White Springs. By permission of the State Archives of Florida.

you wait and see." The reporter thought it odd to hear the young guide using "patter" he felt was "a vestige of the Old South, the stock character of The Negro," even as he also observed that "this has been going on for a long time, long before the Wakulla Springs Lodge was built here." He added that Rainey and the other guides were "[delivering] a descendant of Luke Smith's style"; Smith had developed a "singsong preaching style . . . longer on information and shorter on dramatics, but still a recognizable antique."[19]

The reporter failed to hear the history in that "antique" voice, a voice that native Floridian and *Tampa Bay Times* columnist Jeff Klinkenberg described as being rooted in "a tradition steeped in African American missionary church choirs, chain gang laborers who sang to make the toil bearable, and railroad workers who made up rhymes and rhythms as they shifted track."[20] These African American guides developed their own narratives and made themselves indispensable in a culture that was becoming increasingly homogenized. As Zora Neale Hurston observed when she collected African American folklore in 1930s Florida: "[Their] negroness is being rubbed off by close contact with white culture."[21] Still, Tom Gavin's creation lived on, prompting one reporter to write: "As Wakulla Springs developed into a resort, an understanding seemed to grow between Henry [the fish] and the

Negro guides who operate the glass bottom boats. Today, Henry will not perform for anyone else."[22] These men could take that to the bank.

Rainbow Springs, like Wakulla and Silver Springs, hired African Americans to pilot their boats. Skipper Lockett became so well known for the distinctive chant he created that he cut a record of his performance at the Florida Folk Festival in White Springs. He began working at Rainbow Springs in 1934 doing maintenance and became a glass bottom boat driver in 1936. As he told the author of "The Bard of Rainbow Springs," "Every time I took a ride, I'd photograph in my mind what I saw and the spiel began to churn in me." Part of what he saw was the fish, and he'd deliver a list of all the species in one breath:

> We got large mouth black bass. We got calico bass. We got small mouth bass. Got blue gill, got shell cracker, got sand shuttle, got shiners, got bream, got leopard gar, got mud fish, jackfish, pot fish, more fish. Got red fall perch, got speckled perch, got a neon fish. Got blue shad, got silver shad, got German carp, got copperhead bream, got mud cat, speckled cat, alligator gar, black gar, gold carp; got 'em all right 'chere at Rainbow Springs.

Lockett told the reporter his spiel was a way of "laying down a monument," and indeed it is; a recording is still available at the Florida State Archives. He added that his eloquent chant was "responsible for my eight room house in Dunnellon. It put my daughter Pansy, now married, through A and M College, and now she's a teacher. My daughter Jacqueline Yvonne, she's 12, she's going to Booker T. Washington School, and I'll put her through college, too, if she wants to go."[23]

African American men like George Morgan, Christopher Lightburn, and Jutson Ayers wrestled alligators at the Alligator Farm in St. Augustine in the 1930s or they raced ostriches like Hurricane, the fastest ostrich in the world, over at the Jacksonville Ostrich Farm. A billboard featuring Christopher Lightburn prying open the jaws of an alligator was placed on the road leading into the city. After he was unable to wrestle gators anymore the "Mayor of Lincolnville" started the Lincolnville Festival.[24] Rena Ayers, the widow of his colleague Jutson Ayers, was honored in 2005 as a legendary "House Mother to the Civil Rights Movement" in St. Augustine for, among other activities, opening her house to people who supported desegregation, including a white lawyer who stayed for four years while working on a civil rights case.[25]

St. Augustine Alligator Farm alligator wrestler Christopher Lightburn was featured on a billboard just outside St. Augustine, welcoming tourists. He was also known as the "Mayor of Lincolnville," for his community service in this historic neighborhood established by former slaves in 1866. By permission of Lu Vickers.

Agnes Jones, or "Aunt Aggie," an ex-slave of African–Native American descent, moved in 1883 with her husband Jenkins Jones to Lake City, Florida, where she created her own attraction, known as the Bone Yard, a "weird wonderland" adorned with sculptures and trellises made from animal bones. Between 1900 and 1918 Aunt Aggie's Bone Yard, with its lush vegetable and flower gardens, delighted children and lovers alike, and although there was no admission charge, she made money from selling vegetables and flowers, topped off by tips from visitors. After she passed away her house and gardens were razed and a school for African American children was built on the spot, a "living monument to an ex-slave, who roamed the woods . . . and

Aunt Aggie & her Bone Yard, Lake City, Fla.

"Aunt Aggie" Jones created a bone garden on property she owned with her husband in Lake City, Florida. People came from all over to visit. She also grew flowers and vegetables. By permission of Lu Vickers.

found—in the language of Shakespeare—'tongues in trees, books in the running brooks, sermons in stones and good in everything.'"[26]

Another African American who leaned toward the wild things was Emanuel "Junior" Ruffin, who became "America's only Negro lion tamer" after joining the Clyde Beatty Railroad Circus in 1952, when he was about fourteen years old. Clyde Beatty himself trained Ruffin.[27] When Ruffin joined the Hoxie Brothers Circus, he held "positions of star lion and tiger trainer, adult elephant act trainer, baby elephant act trainer, big top tent boss, lot superintendent, master welder, head truck mechanic and truck driver." Leonard "Hoxie" Tucker told a reporter that when Ruffin retired he had to hire seven men to replace him. Ruffin moved to Miami in 1959 to perform at Jungleland, a park purchased by Beatty. In the early 1990s he helped launch the Univer-Soul Circus, and in 2010 he became the only African American performer ever to be inducted into Sarasota's Circus Ring of Fame."[28]

Some African Americans, like Geder Walker and Dana Dorsey, bought property and launched their own empires. Walker came to Miami from Georgia and built the four-hundred-seat Lyric Theater in 1913. The local paper described it as "possibly the most beautiful and costly playhouse owned by Colored people in all the Southland."[29]

Dorsey, who came to Florida in 1896 to work as a carpenter on Flagler's railroad, bought parcels of land in Colored Town, the area where

Flagler's workers lived, which would later be known as Overtown. By building houses and renting them, then parlaying that income into a real estate empire, he made himself into a millionaire, banker, hotel owner, and philanthropist. He purchased a barrier island where he created a beach for African Americans to use, but in the mid-1920s, due to rising property taxes, he was forced to sell the property to Carl Fisher. Today Fisher Island is known as "America's most exclusive zip code." And yet, as John Dudley wrote on his blog, "Where Is Dana Albert Dorsey?" You won't hear the name of "one of the greatest architects of South Florida buildings" mentioned with Fisher or Flagler or Rockefeller, even though "his achievements were just as great if not greater" since he "owned and sold much of the land that was developed into the multi-million dollar properties of today."[30]

He built the Dorsey Hotel, the first black-owned hotel in Miami. In 1981 the hotel burned down—the victim of blight—and the *Miami News* lamented:

> As it turns out, it was not just another dull useless warehouse that had burned. Nat King Cole had lived there. So had Billy Eckstein and Dinah Washington. The Dorsey was a name hotel during the joyful rich era when Black Overtown was alive and swarming. . . . Another piece of Miami history is gone. And one of its earliest and grandest Black pioneers—D. A. Dorsey—is close to being wiped clean off the face of the city."

Dorsey's stepdaughter Dana Chapman said, "He built the whole hotel himself":

> He did it with black laborers and it took him a while and when he finished it, it was paid for in cash. He didn't owe one cent on it. But you have to remember: He was a black man so he couldn't get financing. And that's the whole part about Overtown that's so exciting. Because it's like *ours*—you know, no place else would they let us stay at that point in time. So we made it the Black mecca of the South.[31]

And just as African Americans were not able to get financing from white-owned banks, and were not allowed to visit the attractions or enjoy the amenities of the hotels and restaurants where they worked, so it went at Silver Springs. Paradise Park is rarely mentioned in histories of Silver Springs. When the Davidson and Ray families sold Silver

Following pages: A group of young boys on a field trip explore the Silver River on the *Tranquilizer*, a jungle cruise boat. Photo by Bruce Mozert. By permission of Bruce Mozert. Courtesy of Cynthia Wilson-Graham.

Visitors from across the country pose for a picture holding bumper stickers that read "Don't Miss Florida's Silver Springs." Photo by Bruce Mozert. By permission of Bruce Mozert. Courtesy of Marion County Black Archives.

Springs to the American Broadcasting Company in 1962, the *Ocala Star Banner* ran an editorial summarizing their legacy to the people of Ocala who "will always hold them in the highest esteem" for "making Silver Springs a thing of quality and joy forever."[32] There was no mention of Paradise Park or the people who found joy at Paradise Park, and that was a disservice, not only to the memory of Paradise Park but also to Carl Ray and Shorty Davidson, who—despite whatever flaws they may have had—founded the park for the African American community.

Tom Cavanaugh, who headed up Florida Leisure Attractions, the management team that came in after ABC sold out in the late 1980s and early 1990s, told a reporter he was familiar with Paradise Park, although the Silver Springs website made no mention of it. "It was a fabulous location," he said. "As you go down Fort King waterway, sitting on the right hand side, you see the giraffes with big oak trees. That's where Paradise Park was. They really had the best part of the park," he added. "That part of history I was never really enthused with because that's not my make-up. In another way, I am glad to see it's no longer there, of course. It's not the way we want to live our lives— separately. I certainly don't."[33]

"South of the South"

In spite of its reputation as a tourist region, [Florida] had been an Old South slave state as well as a stalwart member of the Confederate States of America during the Civil War.

WALTER HOWARD, *LYNCHINGS*

Although African Americans may have had the "best part of the park" at Silver Springs, as Tom Cavanaugh of Florida Leisure Attractions said, the reality is that Florida itself was well known to be unsafe for African Americans even as it promoted itself as the "Land of Sunshine, Oranges and Health."[1] Around the same time that Irving Berlin wrote "Florida by the Sea" in 1925—with the lyrics: "In the lovely land of Florida/Sunny Florida by the sea/All the sunshine in America/Is in Florida you'll agree"—the African American newspaper *Florida Sentinel* published the following "Warning to Negro Tourists":

> Those who have automobiles want to exercise more caution when driving over the State. The small villages and towns are far from civilized and at every opportunity give their savagery full play. The Negro who drives a Ford gets by no better than one who drives a Lincoln. Every one must pay a toll for driving through these small white settlements. You don't have to speed. If you roll along at the rate of four miles an hour, if you happen to be the least colored[,] it is sufficient reason to hold you up and take from you a batch of your cold cash, and on top of that be rough-necked by a man whose nickel-faced badge is his only protection against the charge of high-way robbery.

The editorial went on to explain that the judges and cops in these small towns must rely on tickets for their pay as "the town itself may

The 11th District of the American Legion was composed entirely of African American posts and sponsored the annual "Miss Paradise Park" contest on Labor Day weekend. They used the event to raise money for charitable causes. A soldier blows the whistle as the annual contest begins. Photo by Bruce Mozert. By permission of Bruce Mozert. Courtesy of Cynthia Wilson-Graham.

not afford enough to keep up a razor-back hog." The piece ended with some admonitions including, "Don't leave your city unless you are certain you have enough gas to carry you to the next city."[2]

Gilbert King, author of the Pulitzer Prize–winning book *The Devil in the Grove: Thurgood Marshall, the Groveland Boys, and the Dawn of a New America*, wrote that Florida, at the time Paradise Park opened, still had a "boundless capacity for racial inhumanity" and was "south of the South" but had somehow managed to avoid the "scrutiny" applied to Mississippi and Alabama, even though by 1930 Florida reported more lynchings than any other state. Not only were there more lynchings, but at times whole towns were wiped out.[3] Against this backdrop of violence, the creation of Paradise Park becomes even more meaningful.

In 1920 in Ocoee, Florida, a small town about 115 miles south of Ocala, a racial riot broke out when a black man was barred from voting in the presidential election because he had not paid the poll tax. In the dispute that followed, with shootings on both sides, the riot became a massacre. The town's whites went on a rampage, burning homes, churches, and a lodge and killing at least six African Americans by some accounts, or more than fifty by more recent accounts, including July Perry, who was lynched. Over the years as the number of dead on both sides has been debated, one fact remained clear. Nearly five hundred African Americans left Ocoee shortly after that night, and none returned. With the exception of a couple of blacks listed on the census in 1930, Ocoee was an all-white town up until the 1980s. As late as in 1959 the town had a sign at the city limits that read "Dogs and Negroes Not Welcome."[4] A similar incident took place at Rosewood in 1923, when at least six African Americans were murdered and the entire town was burned to the ground because a white woman accused a black man of rape.

In his book King writes about an infamous case that took place in June 1949, just one month after Paradise Park opened, in the small town of Groveland, about an hour south of Ocala. The Groveland Four, as Ernest Thomas, Charles Greenlee, Samuel Shepherd, and Walter Irvin came to be called, were young African American men falsely accused of raping a young white woman in Groveland. Thomas was immediately tracked down in the woods and killed, and the other three were arrested. A mob swarmed the jail in an attempt to lynch the men. When that failed, they headed to Groveland, where they burned numerous homes, terrorizing the African American families who lived there. Except for the word of the white couple, there was no evidence that the men had done anything wrong.[5]

Edmond Fordham of Ocala said his brother, William Fordham, was one of only three African American lawyers in Florida in 1949 when he went to interview the men at Raiford, the prison where they were held.[6] According to Robert Saunders, field director for the Florida

NAACP in the 1950s, Fordham, who had just completed law school, had set up an office in Tampa. "If you read the history of the Groveland case, you'll find that it was Fordham that went up to Raiford. In questioning the three youths who were up there, he found a lot of blood on the clothes and everything. It was this report from Fordham that opened up the real effort to fully investigate what happened in the Groveland case."[7]

However, partially because evidence that would have proved their innocence was withheld, they were convicted. In April of 1951, the case was overturned by the Supreme Court. Later that year Sam Shepherd was murdered and Irvin was gravely wounded by Sheriff Willis Mc-Call as he was driving them to court. Then, because of his role in the case, Harry Moore and his wife were assassinated. Edmond Fordham said his brother William was also involved with this tragic event. "The sheriff in Lake County, McCall, was a terror," he said. "When Harry Moore's house was bombed my brother was the first person down there."[8]

After Irvin recovered, the trial was moved to Ocala. His lead attorney for the retrial held in Ocala in 1952 was Thurgood Marshall. Besides gaining a retrial for Irvin, Marshall had recently appeared before the Supreme Court to argue that school segregation was a violation of the fourteenth amendment, an argument that culminated in the famous 1954 *Brown v. Board of Education* case. Still, even though Marshall was welcome at the Supreme Court, he wasn't welcome in Bennett's Drug Store in downtown Ocala. Attorney Guy Musleh recalled taking Marshall to lunch at Bennett's with two other lawyers during a recess. "We sat at a table in Bennett's and everyone was looking at us . . . some with very disapproving looks." The lawyers ordered club sandwiches, and when they came, Marshall swapped plates with Musleh. "He said teasingly that if it was being poisoned, someone else would get it."[9] Given the fact that he was under constant threat in Florida, and given what had happened to Harry T. Moore, Marshall had every reason to worry for his life.

Despite Marshall's pleas, Irvin was convicted again and sentenced to death. Former governor LeRoy Collins commuted that to a life sentence in 1955; Irvin was released from prison in 1968 and died just one year later.[10] In September 2012 the families of the four men petitioned Florida Governor Rick Scott to clear their names. They received a letter from the governor's office informing them that they needed to contact the state attorney's office as the governor could not "expunge records."[11]

The Ocoee, Rosewood, and Groveland cases are deadly examples of the discrimination that permeated every aspect of the lives of Florida's African Americans, whether they were rich or poor. As far as tourism or entertainments went, the state played Dr. Jekyll and Mr. Hyde. African Americans made up a large part of the tourism workforce but were excluded from enjoying the attractions where they worked. As for entertainers, from the 1930s to the 1960s stars like Duke Ellington, Cab Calloway, Count Basie, and Sam Cooke played in segregated Miami Beach nightclubs but weren't allowed to sleep in whites only hotels. Josephine Baker famously refused ever to perform in the United States again after being "crudely hounded out of two East Side hotels" in New York. She planned to skip America completely for her 1950–51 tour, but was contacted through her agent by Ned Schuyler, co-owner of Copa City, the famous nightclub in Miami, who offered her good money to do a show there. When told that the club did not allow African Americans inside, she refused. Schuyler then flew to Havana to meet her in person, literally begging her to change her mind. "I have been told that Negroes cannot go to nightclubs in Miami Beach," she told him. "I cannot work where my people cannot go. It's as simple as that." She finally relented when the owners agreed to add a clause to her contract stipulating that there would be no discrimination against any patrons no matter what race.[12] Baker's one-woman protest led several other prominent Miami night clubs to adopt similar policies, prompting the editors of *Ebony* to write:

> It was inevitable that eventually the nauseating bigotry of the South would result in revulsion among Northerners in Miami. The forces of democracy are slow and plodding but as certain of victory as was the tortoise over the hare. Today in Miami a slow but sure revolution seems to be in the making and seemingly for the first time since the Civil War, the North is establishing a beachhead of democracy in the South. Miami is that beachhead.[13]

For years, Miami officials required the city's tourism workforce to carry official identification cards. These rules applied to everyone, white or black, but African Americans were routinely stopped for checks. In the 1930s Iona Holmes worked as a maid at the Mayfair Hotel, where a sign posted in the lobby read "No dogs, no Jews, No coloreds." Jews had it bad, Ms. Holmes recalled decades later, but blacks had it worse. "We couldn't even use the toilets in the hotel where we worked," she said. "If we had to go to the bathroom during our 8 hour shift, we had to walk three blocks away to another hotel that had a special servants' bathroom for blacks—even when it was raining. We couldn't drink a glass of water at the hotel. Had to go outside to use a public water fountain, one that said 'Coloreds.'"[14]

Heavyweight world champion Joe Louis fought before a segregated audience in Jacksonville a couple of months before Paradise Park opened in 1949. One consolation for the crowd, as a newspaper reported, was the Brown Bomber's generous ringside announcement: "Negro fans were invited to be his guests at a colored bar after the bout . . . and [he] picked up a sizable bill."[15] In the early sixties, "when neither money nor fame was enough to secure them a room at most hotels in town," Malcolm X, a young Muhammad Ali, and Martin Luther King Jr. frequented the Hampton House Motel in Brownsville, a black community near Miami Beach. In 1964 Ali, or Cassius Clay as he was then known, told a crowd at the Hampton that he was going to "whoop" Sonny Liston, and he did, then went back and ate a big bowl of ice cream to celebrate—at the segregated motel.[16] The Hampton House, originally named Booker Terrace, was built in 1953 by Harry

Hampton House in Miami was the place to be in the 1950s and 1960s. Today the motel is being renovated to become a museum. By permission of Lu Vickers.

Girls in the Miss Paradise Park beauty contest wave to Bruce Mozert as he photographs them walking across the stage. Thousands attended the park for the annual Labor Day beauty pageant; many of the visitors were from out of town. Photo by Bruce Mozert. By permission of Bruce Mozert. Courtesy of Cynthia Wilson-Graham.

and Florence Markowitz and renovated and renamed in 1961. Martin Luther King Jr. is said to have practiced his 1963 "I Have a Dream" speech at the motel. However, Hampton House suffered when desegregation came and by 2013 was "just a frame being held up by some sticks," according to Miami preservationist Enid Pinkney. In early 2000 she headed up a group to save the iconic motel and formed the Historic Hampton House Community Trust.[17] By June 2014 the roof had been repaired, and restoration continues to turn the motel into a "music museum and local cultural center."[18]

Against the deeply troubled backdrop of Florida's segregationist history, fourteen years after Carl Ray and Shorty Davidson bought the original Paradise Park, on Emancipation Day, May 20, 1949, they opened Paradise Park for African Americans. The day before the opening Ray and his son Buck took the Marion County commissioners and some other Ocala officials down to the attraction to see the beach, bathhouse, and pavilion. They looked over the swimming area and the dock where patrons could board the glass bottom boats for a ride over the springs.[19] Opening day was announced with a small advertisement in area newspapers, including the *Ocala Banner,* and in the *Daytona Beach Morning Journal*:

> NOW! Colored Folks Can See Florida's Silver Springs from Exclusive Paradise Park. Ride Glass Bottomed boats . . . See Ross Allen's great collection of snakes . . . Swim in the world's clearest water . . . Picnic in a ten acre park . . . Enjoy delicious food, candy, soft drinks . . . Free Admission . . . Exclusively for Colored Persons.[20]

On opening day, buses were scheduled to pick up visitors at Covenant Missionary Baptist Church every hour all day. Various preachers would be on hand to oversee the program, including the Rev. J. E. McCrary, whose son Jesse McCrary, a Howard Academy graduate and civil rights activist, would go on to become Florida's first African American secretary of state. Reverend Oliver Pinkston, the father of civil rights activist Frank Pinkston and himself a civil rights activist, was also on hand to "extend a welcome from Silver Springs." The featured speaker was Dr. Lee Royal Hampton. Reverend Gardner of St. Paul Baptist announced that his church planned "a big celebration for the opening."[21]

The celebrations would continue for the next twenty years, beginning with the first anniversary celebration in 1950, when Florida A&M's renowned coach Jake Gaither would appear on the program with Althea Gibson, then a freshman tennis player, who just six years later would become the first African American to win the Grand Slam.[22] In 1957 she became the first African American to win Wimbledon and shake the hand of Queen Elizabeth. "Shaking hands with the queen of England," she wrote later, "was a long way from being forced to sit in the colored section of the bus going into downtown Wilmington, N.C."[23]

7

Segregated Summers

Summer resorts maintain the color line perhaps more rigidly than any other American institution. From Palm Springs, California, to Palm Beach, Florida, extends a stretch of "Caucasian Only" and "Restricted Clientele" signs on vacation spots. . . . However, legislation and education have broken barriers at many places and the number of summer hotels and camps that will admit Negroes is going up. . . . But because most colored pleasure seekers are not anxious to tilt with Jim Crow—at least during their vacation—nearby Negro resorts still attract the most vacationists.

EBONY, JULY 1947

Long before Shorty Davidson and Carl Ray decided to open Paradise Park, African Americans obviously sought safe places to enjoy their summertime leisure. And during Reconstruction, they had the law on their side. The Civil Rights Act of 1875 guaranteed "the full and equal enjoyment of any of the accommodations, advantages, facilities, and privileges of inns, public conveyances on land or water, theaters and other places of public amusement; subject only to the conditions and limitations established by law, and applicable alike to citizens of every race and color."[1]

As noted scholar and historian W.E.B. DuBois wrote in *Black Reconstruction in America*:

[This period] was the Golden Dawn, after chains of a thousand years. . . . For the first time in their life, they could travel; they could see; they could change the dead level of their labor; they could talk to friends and sit at sundown and in moonlight, listening and imparting wonder-tales. . . . They need not fear the patrol; they need not even cringe before a white face, and touch their hats.[2]

In the years immediately following Emancipation, according to historian Lawrence Levine, former slaves seized on the opportunity to travel: "Even those who would not or could not leave their homes permanently manifested the need to take advantage of one of the chief fruits of freedom, and railway excursions became an important part of Black social life." These excursions were usually organized by churches or fraternal organizations.[3] Even though African Americans initially enjoyed some mobility, the ease of traveling did not last long. By 1883 the Supreme Court had demolished the Civil Rights Act of 1875, determining that the fourteenth amendment did not provide Congress with the power to stop discrimination practiced by individual citizens and referring the ruling back to the states, which by this point were creating laws that established segregation, most commonly in schools but also in other facilities.[4]

With the passage of a law in 1887, Florida was the first state to begin requiring that railway companies provide separate cars for blacks and whites, and other states quickly followed suit.

After Louisiana passed a similar law in 1890, African Americans organized a "Citizens' Committee to Test the Constitutionality of the Separate Car Law." Homer Plessy boarded an East Coast Rail train and got arrested for refusing to move into the "colored" car. The group then filed suit. *Plessy v. Ferguson* worked its way to the Supreme Court in 1896 and ended in a ruling that justified segregation in "transportation, public accommodations, and schools," a decision that remained in place until overruled by the 1954 *Brown v. Board of Education* decision.[5] And even then it was years, and in some cases decades, before the ruling took full effect. Some would argue that it still has not taken full effect.

Despite Florida's early entry into segregating trains, as C. Vann Woodward noted in *The Strange Career of Jim Crow* (a book Martin Luther King Jr. referred to as "the historical bible of the Civil Rights movement"): "One of the strangest things about the career of Jim Crow was that the system was born in the North and reached an advanced age before moving South in force."[6]

In Asbury Park, New Jersey, as early as 1885, African American hotel workers and white tourists often found themselves side by side on the beaches at the resort founded by James Bradley. However, that didn't last long. In 1887, when Bradley made negative comments about

"the way the beach seats and plaza are monopolized by the colored help of the hotels and cottages," he was met with powerful resistance from Reverend John Francis Robinson, who told a crowd gathered in protest:

> We colored people fought for our liberty some years ago and we do not propose to be denied it at this late day . . . we fought to save the Union as the white man did. This country is for the whites and blacks alike, including the beach of Asbury Park. We shall go to the beach when we please because we have a right there.[7]

By 1889, citing their "[unwillingness] to swim in the Roman bath or in the surf next to a swarthy African and his best girl, or to be crowded while strolling on the plaza by the waiter who serves them at meals," and calling the situation "intolerable," a group petitioned Bradley to "[exclude] the intruders from the beach during the fashionable hours of the day," and by 1896 Jim Crow segregation was in effect.[8] As David Goldberg wrote, this was a moment when "the rhetoric of equality and moral superiority was thus abandoned by white politicians and northern citizens, who, in the aftermath of Reconstruction's collapse, sought to publicly and commercially separate themselves from their fellow black citizens."[9]

At the turn of the twentieth century a group of African American women and men swim in the Atlantic Ocean at Asbury Park, New Jersey. By permission of Lu Vickers.

Segregated Summers   101

Martin Luther King Jr. with a friend at Chicken Bone Beach in New Jersey. Photo by John Mosley. By permission of Temple University.

Some of the most violent racial clashes in the North were triggered by incidents on beaches. In 1912 an African American child was attacked for trying to swim at the 39th Street beach in Chicago, and police intervened to prevent mob violence. There was no stopping the violence in 1919 when a teenager named Eugene Williams drifted from the segregated 31st Street beach to the 29th Street beach on Lake Michigan. He was drowned and a riot broke out, lasting for a week, resulting in thirty-eight deaths, and leaving a thousand people homeless, mostly African Americans. This riot was but one that occurred in what came to be known as the "Red Summer," the peak of racial violence instigated by whites during the great migration of African Americans to the north.[10]

Around 1900 in Atlantic City, New Jersey, white hotel owners "pushed black beach-goers from the fronts of their establishments down to the Missouri Avenue beach south of the Million Dollar Pier," to cater to tourists from the South.[11] The beach eventually became known as Chicken Bone Beach, the "largest de facto segregated beach on the Jersey shore." Although some felt the nickname was racist, Muriel Greenwich, who lived nearby, explained: "They came in with their pots of collard greens and chicken and all sorts of Southern cuisine, and as a result, they needed some place to eat it, so they ate it on the beach."[12]

Chicken Bone Beach might have begun out of the painful reality of segregation, but like Paradise Park, it quickly grew into a place to see and be seen. According to Lorenzo Langford of the Atlantic City Council, "You used to see everybody at Chicken Bone Beach. All the greats that came to town—Duke Ellington, Sammy Davis Jr. said it was their favorite place in the city to hang out."[13]

And there are photographs to prove it. John Mosley, a self-taught photographer from Philadelphia, captured three decades of African American history in both Philadelphia and Atlantic City. According to Leslie Willis-Lowry, archivist of the Blockson Collection at the Temple University library that houses Mosley's large archive, "It was Mosley's intention to represent his proud heritage and to rightfully portray African-Americans in a positive manner during a difficult time of racism and segregation." His photographs show a people at play, relaxing within a circle of friends and family, safe from danger: Martin Luther King Jr. decked out in beach attire on Chicken Bone Beach; heavyweight champ Joe Louis relaxing with friends; Sammy Davis Jr. cavorting with a woman in his arms; and groups of children playing in the sand.[14]

Crisis magazine, created in 1910 by the NAACP and edited by W.E.B. Dubois, had always included travel information and advertisements for boarding houses and hotels that catered to African Americans. But the publication that best addressed the need for safe places to travel and to take care of other business was *The Negro Traveler's Green Book*, a guide launched in 1936 by Harlem postal worker Victor Green. He initially created the *Green Book* for use in New York City, but the response was so overwhelming that by the following year he went national. Julian Bond, longtime civil rights activist and politician, who got a chance to play Victor Green in Calvin Alexander Ramsay's play titled *The Green Book*, told NPR reporter Neal Conan that his family used the book every time they traveled—and not just in the South: "Segregation reached everywhere in the United States, and even though the laws didn't require it, it was practiced almost everywhere."

Bond added that the book did more than list resorts; it listed taverns, beauty parlors, barber shops, and tourist homes. "You think about the things that most travelers take for granted, or most people today take for granted," he said. "If I go to New York City and want a hair cut, it's pretty easy for me to find a place where that can happen, but it wasn't easy then. White barbers would not cut black people's hair. White beauty parlors would not take black women as customers—hotels and so on, down the line. You needed the *Green Book* to tell you where you can go without having doors slammed in your face."[15]

Green himself predicted that one day his book would become an anachronism. "There will be a day sometime in the near future when this guide will not have to be published. That is when we as a race will have equal opportunities and privileges in the United States."[16] However, the book continued to be published for almost thirty years, until 1964, well into the era of sit-ins and protests.

In 1946 W. H. Butler began publishing the *Travelguide* for black vacationers, with the motto "Vacation and Recreation without Humiliation." According to historian Susan Rugh, Butler's guide was more "racially assertive," not only because of its motto but because "it reminded readers that they should take a active role in fighting racial discrimination."[17] Rugh's book *Are We There Yet?* pulled testimony from complaints that traveling African Americans sent to the NAACP. She said that in the 1950s these vacationers were essentially "foot soldiers" for the NAACP, reporting the discrimination they experienced all over the United States. "Those who pushed the Civil Rights Act forward used such images of the vacationing family having to sleep in their car after being turned away by hotel managers," Rugh told a reporter. "They were trying to appeal to senators who took vacations with their families. This was supposedly the Golden Age of American family vacations, but it was not so for black families."[18]

The *Travelguide*, edited by W. H. "Billy" Butler, included information on civil rights legislation and encouraged travelers to report abuses to the NAACP. From the New York Public Library. Courtesy of Susan Rugh.

Indeed, as Eddie Vereen pointed out to a reporter in 1956, racism had economic repercussions for whites as well. "White people are inclined to forget that the Negro tourist and traveler plays an important role in the economy of this state and we are definitely not meeting their needs. Every time a Negro motorist must sleep in his automobile or eat beside the road we are losing potential tourist income." At that time Ocala had only one "tourist court and one hotel catering to Negroes and they [could] take less than 50 visitors a night"—and Paradise Park was bringing in half a dozen busloads of people per day. "I sometimes spend as much time in hunting rooms as I do in managing this park," Vereen said. "It sure does look like someone is losing a good bet for a profitable business in not establishing more accommodations for Negroes." Vereen seemed to be taking a page from Booker T. Washington when he spoke to the reporter, assuring him that most Negroes did not want widespread integration. This was two years after the *Brown v. Board of Education* decision. Ocala would struggle with federal courts over integration all the way into the '90s. "But," Vereen concluded, "we don't like to be forced to sleep along the side of the road simply because the Negro's place as a tourist and traveler has not been recognized."[19]

Sylvia Jones said her Uncle Eddie would find homes for people to stay in "when they came from out of town to visit the park. Ms. Margaret Palmer would keep people sometimes; she was a neighbor of ours. That's one of the reasons why Dr. Lamb opened his hotel. There was only one black motel, the Wimberly Motel on Ft. King Street."[20] It wasn't just people visiting Paradise Park who needed places to stay. Amelia "Ann" Pinkston, whose family was active in civil rights and was

A group of Pull-man sleeping car porters visit Paradise Park. Photo by Bruce Mozert. By permission of Bruce Mozert. Courtesy of Marion County Black Archives.

one of the pioneer black families in Silver Springs, recalled that white families would come to town to see Silver Springs and would room at the Shalimar Motel. However, there was no place for the African American maids and chauffeurs who accompanied them to stay, so they would board with the Pinkston family.[21]

"Black people, while visiting Paradise Park, could not stay in any of the white-owned hotels in Silver Springs," said Mary Carolyn Williams, whose husband Sam Williams became Ocala's second African American police chief in 2003. "When Dr. Lamb built the Bali Motel, black people could rest there comfortably. There were also rooming houses (long and short term) which were available in our community. Annually, in December, a large Church Conference was held at a church on Fort King and Academy Street. Many of the people would stay in the homes of families living in the surrounding neighborhood."[22]

Girl Scouts set up tents for a day trip at Paradise Park. Photo by Bruce Mozert. By permission of Bruce Mozert. Courtesy of Marion County Black Archives.

A large group
gathers for a
picnic on the
grounds of
Paradise Park.
Photo by Bruce
Mozert. By
permission of
Bruce Mozert.
Courtesy of
Marion County
Black Archives.

Dr. Ernest Lamb had opened the Carmen Manor Motel in the early 1950s—it appears in the 1956 edition of the *Green Book*. In October 1960, just a few years after Vereen made his comments, Lamb opened the Bali Motor Inn next to his already established Club Bali. Lamb's slogan was: "Only the best is good enough for you," and he advertised the establishment as the "newest, most fabulous club-motel in the South," a luxurious inn where patrons could visit the Club Bali to get "drinks . . . accurately mixed by a licensed bartender."[23] Lonnie Bunch, director of the National Museum of African American History and Culture at the Smithsonian, said the *Green Book* was still necessary in the 1960s even as people protested against discrimination, since segregation was still a part of their regular lives. "The 'Green Book' tried to provide a tool to deal with those situations," he told the *New York Times*. "It also allowed families to protect their children, to help them ward off those horrible points at which they might be thrown out or not permitted to sit somewhere. It was both a defensive and a proactive mechanism."[24]

Educator Juanita Cunningham—an elegant woman whose husband James was the first black president of the Ocala City Council and whose family owned the Cunningham Funeral Home, the "largest minority owned business in Marion County"—said she did everything she could "to prevent my children from going through the experiences that I had had all my lifetime. We were in McCrory's," she said in a short documentary film, "and my son, who was six at that time, wanted to use the restroom. I refused to carry him across the street to the courthouse. I ran him back home so he could go to the bathroom, and en route home, he said to me, 'Mama, won't you be glad when co-operation comes?' I said, 'Yes, Jim, I will be happy when things are desegregated.' He knew why I wouldn't take him to the courthouse. I was not going to take him into that colored toilet."[25]

Journalist Thelma Parker recalled a similar transgression that took place at Kennedy's Men's Store, a store she frequently patronized. When she asked a clerk if she could take her three-year-old grandson to the bathroom, she was told there was no bathroom and that she should go elsewhere. She went home, then headed back to the store, where she told the owner, "Take my name off your books as of now. I will not buy anything else from you." Parker's daughter Rosalind Parker Thomas used to sneak out of her house to attend mass meetings in Ocala. "I really was afraid," Thelma Parker said of her daughter's activism, "because people were so mean, you never knew what they were going to do. Naturally, she wasn't afraid."[26]

In April 1963, just a few months before the March on Washington, Roy Wilkins testified before Congress on the difficulties that still existed in traveling while black:

I invite the members of this committee to imagine themselves darker in color and to plan an auto trip from Norfolk, Virginia to the Gulf Coast of Mississippi. How far would you drive each day? Where and under what conditions can you and your family eat? Where can they use a restroom? Can you stop after a reasonable day at the wheel, or must you drive until you reach a city where relatives or friends will accommodate you for the night? Will your children be denied an ice cream cone because they are not white?[27]

Filmmaker and historian Kenneth Jones—who wrote and directed the docudrama *Rosewood*, depicting the 1923 massacre in that Florida African American town essentially burned to the ground—pointed out one result of this discrimination: "Across the South and our country, there were vibrant African American business and cultural areas that thrived during the institutional hatred of racism and segregation. They were very enriching and nourishing economic, business and cultural islands that sat in towns and cities where racism's ugliness thrived. In these areas for the most part, African Americans' dignity, self-worth and joy was less challenged and these cultural islands prospered as their communities were a bedrock of their hope for a better day."[28]

These "cultural islands" included beaches and lakes and resorts like the "Black Pearl" of Atlantic Beach, South Carolina, and Azurest and Nineveh on Sag Harbor in Long Island, where a group of "black whalers" built cottages, some of which are still "in the hands of black families" today.[29] Novelist Colson Whitehead, in his semi-autobiographical novel *Sag Harbor*, wrote via Benji, his teenage protagonist, "We knew where our neighborhood began because that's where the map ended. The black part of town was off in the margins."[30]

Some neighborhoods weren't in the margins at all. Comprising nearly three thousand acres, the "Black Eden" of Idlewild, Michigan, was "the go to spot in Michigan . . . the town that segregation built." According to National Public Radio, "In the 1950s and '60s, Idlewild was just what working-class blacks were looking for: a resort that was reasonable driving distance from places like Chicago, St. Louis and Detroit—yet invisible enough so black Americans could retreat from the ugliness of discrimination and Jim Crow." Today it is listed as a National Historic Register Community.[31]

Other vacation spots included Fox Lake in Indiana, Lake Placid in Missouri, and Lake Elsinore in Riverside, California. In the 1940s African American surfer Nick Gabaldon rode waves at the Ink Well in Santa Monica, California; the Ink Well of Oak Bluffs on Martha's Vineyard has been home to America's black elite from the nineteenth

A young woman rests in the sand at the Ink Well, the African American beach in Santa Monica, California. By permission of Lu Vickers.

century to today.[32] Madame C. J. Walker and Martin Luther King Jr. vacationed there; Spike Lee owns a home there; Henry Louis Gates Jr. vacations there, as have President Obama and his family. Oak Bluffs on Martha's Vineyard began as meeting ground for religious revivals as early as 1834, attracting both African Americans and whites. One of the first inns built for and by African Americans was the Shearer Cottage, constructed by Charles and Henrietta Shearer in 1912 and still in operation today.[33]

Highland Beach was developed in Maryland by Charles Douglass, son of abolitionist Frederick Douglass. The younger Douglass and his wife had been refused service at the Bay Ridge Resort on the Chesapeake Bay and ended up staying at a nearby boarding house owned by an African American couple, Charles and Charity Brashears. The Brashears were also farmers, and they owned property on Chesapeake Bay, which they sold to Douglass. In 1892, with backing from his father, Douglass created a "privatopia" for prominent African Americans including Harriet Tubman, W.E.B. Dubois, Booker T. Washington, and Paul Robeson.[34]

Picnickers from Camp Clarissa Scott, a YWCA camp named after the writer and poet Clarissa Scott Delaney, at Highland Beach, Maryland, in 1931. Charles Douglass, son of abolitionist Frederick Douglass, founded Highland Beach in the 1890s. Photo by Addison Scurlock. By permission of the Scurlock Studio Records, Archives Center, National Museum of American History, Smithsonian Institution.

Charles built a large house he called "Twin Oaks" overlooking the bay for his father, but the elder Douglass passed away before he could enjoy it. According to the *New York Times*, other African American getaways sprung up nearby, including "Arundel-on-the-Bay, Oyster Harbor and Bay Highlands, along with Columbia Beach, farther down. They constituted a southern outpost for blacks of education and means, who up north frequented Oak Bluffs on Martha's Vineyard."[35]

Before she was a visitor to Highland Beach, Harriet Tubman, who had escaped slavery in Maryland, went to the resort town of Cape May, where she worked as a maid and cook at the Congress Hotel. She is said to have used her wages to help fund runaway slave travel on the

Underground Railway.[36] By the late 1870s other African Americans visited Cape May to vacation at the Banneker Hotel, and by 1911 they were welcome at the Hotel Dale. A small ad in the *Crisis* described it as "the finest and most complete hostelry in the United States for our race."[37]

Clearly, segregation extended beyond the southern states. The city of Manhattan Beach near Los Angeles forced the closure of Bruce's Beach in the 1920s. Charles and Willa Bruce had bought property on the Pacific Ocean in 1912 and quickly turned it into a resort for African Americans, complete with a dance hall, café, and inn. The resort didn't last long. The KKK burned crosses on the property and tried to set the inn on fire. Then the city took official action, using eminent domain to force the Bruces out.[38] In 2007 the city of Manhattan Beach gave the park back its original name and placed a plaque on site: "This two-block neighborhood was home to several minority families and was condemned through eminent domain proceedings commenced in 1924. Those tragic circumstances reflected the views of a different time." At the dedication ceremony Bernard Bruce, the founders' grandson, said: "When I told folks that my family once owned the beach here, they would laugh at me. They didn't believe African Americans owned beaches."[39]

Farther south in North Carolina was Freeman Beach, owned for more than 150 years by the descendants of Alexander Freeman, a free man of color who moved into the area in the mid-nineteenth century and began a fishing business. By 1876 his son Robert had bought more than 2,400 acres and began selling parcels to other families. In the 1920 his heirs developed a portion of the land and built a hotel known as the SeaBreeze. The beachfront continued to be called Freeman Beach, but the area surrounding the SeaBreeze took its name and was soon populated with other hotels, restaurants, cottages, and so many juke joints—thirty-one by one count—that it became known as "Bop City." African American musicians like Ike and Tina Turner and James Brown played in Wilmington but spent the night in one of the hotels at Freeman's Beach.

SeaBreeze/Freeman Beach, like a lot of other black-owned or black-managed leisure spots, including Paradise Park, suffered when desegregation made it possible for the patrons to go to other attractions. Not only that, but family-owned or "heirs' properties" are susceptible to loss as a result of being passed down to many descendants, or "fractionalized," as the African American Environmentalist Association described it, and thus became prey to land developers.[40] Add two hurricanes into the mix, and you can wash away a place that used to be "like the Strip in Las Vegas," according to Barbara Dinkins, who visited the beach when she was a teenager in the 1960s. "Anything could happen." Today Freeman Beach is known as Freeman Park, and SeaBreeze still exists—with some of the original landowners.[41]

South Carolina was most famously home to Atlantic Beach, or the "Black Pearl," as it came to be known. The beachfront property was purchased in the 1930s by an African American man named George Tyson, the story goes, to provide a place for the maids and cooks of white landowners who wanted them to have somewhere to go on their days off. An orange rope was anchored in the Atlantic Ocean to mark the dividing line between the white beach and the black beach. After running into financial difficulties in the 1940s, Tyson engaged the help of some friends, a group of doctors, lawyers, and other professionals, who formed the Atlantic Beach Company. The Black Pearl then became a thriving community and in 1966 received a state charter making its designation as a "black owned beach" official.[42] Still, desegregation had a negative effect, and by 2009 the "leading ocean resort for blacks up and down the East Coast," where Marvin Gaye and Otis Redding once played, was almost a ghost town.[43] Today the town's website has a call for renewal: "Atlantic Beach still struggles to exist and awaits the return of the African-American family, the family she rolled out the red carpet for, when Blacks were forbidden to enter other beaches. Abandoned by her own, Atlantic Beach shall rise again in spite of all that has happened through the years."[44]

8

Divided Beaches

So long as the Gulf Stream flows up the East Coast of Florida—so long as the sun shines—the East Coast of Florida will be the most natural place to spend the winter.

FLORIDA EAST COAST RAILWAY ADVERTISEMENT, 1926

It shall be unlawful for any white person or persons to bathe together with any negro person or persons, or for negro person or persons to bathe together with any white person or persons in the waters of the Atlantic Ocean within the limits of the City of Pablo Beach."

ORDINANCE IN PABLO BEACH, FLORIDA, 1924

Florida, with its immense coastline, was home to few and far between swimming areas for African Americans, whether the Gulf of Mexico, Atlantic Ocean, swimming pool, lake, or river. There would be no orange ropes anchored in the Atlantic, as there were in South Carolina. As late as 1955 the Sarasota County Commission threatened to sell its beaches to "private operators" in order to "prevent Negroes from using [them.]"[1] African Americans had to fight for the right to swim in the state's waters. The most famous of the beaches accessible to black people were the African American–owned American Beach on Amelia Island and Virginia Key in Miami, both of which were on the Atlantic. Some were decidedly smaller, as at Lake Stella in Crescent City, the small town near Palatka where *Tampa Bay Times* columnist Bill Maxwell grew up. Also an investigative reporter, Maxwell wrote an essay for "Parallel Lives," a project about growing up in segregated Florida. Beverly Coyle wrote the white version and Maxwell, titling his contribution "Angry Young Man," wrote about growing up black. He was born in Fort Lauderdale to farmworker parents who had to leave Broward County in search of work after the bean crop was destroyed by too much rain. On their way to Virginia they dropped Maxwell off in Crescent City with his grandparents. He had some rough times—to put it lightly—and he recalled how the "vast differences" between the worlds of black and white were displayed particularly at Lake Stella, where all the town's children congregated in the summer.

> We assumed that Mother Nature had drawn a line across the 308-acre lake, separating the white side from the Negro side. We swam and played on the "Babylon side"—named for the community that was home to the Negro grave yard—and whites used the "Whitesville side." It had white sand, which the town provided on its shore. Our side was grassy and muddy and dotted with the shells of mussels that washed ashore.[2]

He also swam at Paradise Park. "Paradise Park was wonderful," he said, "but it wasn't the same for me because I had been on the Atlantic Ocean and there is nothing like the Atlantic Ocean. The Silver River was cold and there was a current to it so it wasn't like the real beach. And neither was Lake Stella. But I understood. I was also a migrant farmworker and we went up and down the east coast from Fort Lauderdale to Poughkeepsie, New York, and we stayed in places like Virginia and Delaware so I got a chance to see the Atlantic Ocean as a kid. We couldn't go to those white beaches in those other states. What we did was find spots where we could sneak down to the ocean. That's what we did; we had these makeshift beaches. Paradise Park was a big deal because it was the only place in the whole area we could go, but we did sneak into the Atlantic Ocean over there in St. Augustine. We found some places we could get in. I think the whites knew we were doing it and didn't bother us because we weren't near them."[3]

Some areas where African Americans could swim and relax were so off the beaten path that very little is known about them now. Milwaukee Springs in Alachua County was a "colored only" recreation spot that opened some time in the 1940s. During World War II a group proposed that the site be turned over to the army so that Florida's African American soldiers would have a place to wind down when not training at nearby camps.[4]

The Popular Beach at Paradise Park
On Silver River near Ocala, Florida

Children play in the water and others bask in the sun while sightseers enjoy the popular beach at Paradise Park. Photo by Bruce Mozert. By permission of Bruce Mozert. Courtesy of Cynthia Wilson-Graham.

Sunbathing is Fun
at Paradise Park on Silver River
near Ocala, Florida

SILVER SPRINGS
FROM
PARADISE PARK
FOR COLORED PEOPLE

ING GLASS BOTTOMED BOAT RIDE
WATERS OF SILVER SPRINGS

Above: Luresa Lake sunbathes on one of the famous horseshoe palms growing along the Silver River. Photo by Bruce Mozert. By permission of Bruce Mozert. Courtesy of Cynthia Wilson-Graham.

Right: The outside of a Paradise Park brochure featuring the glass bottom boat and a photo of Luresa Lake. By permission of Cynthia Wilson-Graham.

The Glass-Bottom Boat Trip from Paradise Park
On Silver River near Ocala, Florida

A group of young women sunbathe at Paradise Park
as a glass bottom boat passes by in the background on
this postcard. Photo by Bruce Mozert. By permission of
Bruce Mozert. Courtesy of Cynthia Wilson-Graham.

Willie Marsh, one of the first boat captains at Silver Springs, said that sometimes people got so excited feeding the fish their false teeth would fall into the river. By permission of Lu Vickers.

Left to right: Arlene Sims, Joyce Johnson, Lillian Vereen, Alfronia Johnson, and Luresa Lake pet and feed the tame deer at Paradise Park. Photo by Bruce Mozert. By permission of Bruce Mozert. Courtesy of Cynthia Wilson-Graham.

Admiring one of the snakes at Ross Allen's Reptile Exhibit at Paradise Park are Luresa Lake (*right*), Lillian Vereen (*behind snake*), and friends. Photo by Bruce Mozert. By permission of Bruce Mozert. Courtesy of Cynthia Wilson-Graham.

Alligator "Old Coochie" at Paradise Park
On Silver River near Ocala, Florida

Bill Johnson, who worked with the alligators, is pictured here with "Old Coochie" on one of the postcards from Paradise Park. Photo by Bruce Mozert. By permission of Bruce Mozert. Courtesy of Cynthia Wilson-Graham.

Above: The glass bottom boats were one of the main attractions at Paradise Park. Lillian Vereen (*center*) and other riders look into eighty feet of water while riding down the river. Photo by Bruce Mozert. By permission of Bruce Mozert. Courtesy of Cynthia Wilson-Graham.

Right: Reginald Lewis, grandson of Eddie Vereen, was featured in one of the ink blotters advertising Paradise Park. Photo by Leroy Roundtree. Courtesy of Cynthia Wilson-Graham.

No Wonder I'm Smiling!
I've Seen
SILVER SPRINGS
from the
GLASS BOTTOMED BOATS
at FLORIDA'S PARADISE PARK
ON FLORIDA ROAD 40
SPECIAL RATES FOR SCHOOL AND CHURCH GROUPS

Milwaukee Springs was a recreation area in Alachua County near Gainesville, originally created as a camp for African American boys. There is evidence it might have been used as a recreation area for African American soldiers in the 1940s. Photo by Charles Foster. By permission of the State Archives of Florida.

The Delray Beach city commission chartered buses to "take its Negroes to a public Negro beach north of West Palm," rather than allow them to swim at the city's beach.[5] Palm Beach County was pressured into buying beach property ten miles north of West Palm by "both White and Negro posts of the American Legion and Veterans of Foreign Wars." The result was Jupiter Beach and Park.[6] Little Talbot Island, outside Jacksonville, had one beach for both blacks and whites.

The black side was run by Bill Cowley, a Jacksonville businessman and former Atlantic Coast Railroad "dining car steward."[7]

Residents of Newtown in Sarasota fought for decades for a beach, only to be told in 1955 that the city wanted to build them a swimming pool instead. One of the commissioners at the meeting told the disgruntled crowd of African Americans who had gathered to protest, "I didn't come out here to ram a swimming pool down your throats. But we felt you would be more satisfied with a swimming pool where you don't have to be worried about jellyfish and sting-rays." After the laughter died down, an African American man took the floor to respond: "If you white folks can put up with those jelly fish and sting-ray I think maybe we people can put up with them too."[8]

Although the beaches in Fort Lauderdale were initially open to all, by the late 1920s the institution of Jim Crow stopped that. In the 1920s in Broward County groups of African Americans tried to use the beaches at Fort Lauderdale. In an article titled "Use of Beach by Negroes Is to Be Stopped," the *Fort Lauderdale Daily News* reported that rich white property owners objected to the "negroes using the ocean sands in front of their place for holiday frolics" and that city officials were alarmed at the prospect of "cars crowded with Negroes in bathing suits." Although the commissioners apparently felt that blacks were "entitled" to a spot on the beach, they made sure police directed black beachgoers to an area north of the city now known as Galt's Ocean Mile. When Galt's Ocean Mile was bought by a developer in the 1950s African Americans were left beachless. After World War II, when soldiers returned home, citizens felt a renewed sense of urgency, and a group approached the Broward County Commission, petitioning them to provide a "public bathing beach for colored people in Broward County."[9]

Nothing happened for a year. Then in 1946 Dr. Von Mizell, the first African American surgeon in Broward County and the founding president of the Broward NAACP, petitioned for the creation of a beach for Negro citizens. It took seven years before the commission acquiesced. It just so happened that the new beach was a "swampy, out-of-the-way site just south of Port Everglades. It was inaccessible by road and could only be reached by ferryboat." Dr. Mizell protested again—for seven more years—until finally, with the help of activist Eula Johnson, in 1961 people staged a "wade-in" at the white beach off Las Olas

Boulevard.[10] Johnson has been called "Fort Lauderdale's version of Rosa Parks" and was a civil rights activist her entire life, risking her life to advance the cause.[11] She once got between a deputy's shotgun and a young protester during a picket at a segregated theater. She later said, "Fear is a mean monster. I asked God to take away the fear from me. Fear is what kept black people down."[12]

Dr. Mizell faced death as well. His daughter Deborah remembers being whisked away when the Klan showed up at her grandmother's house to "kill a Mizell." She still recalls the burning cross they left behind. On the day of the wade-in, she said, the protesters "walked through a group of police officers and got into the water. They were in there for about 30 to 45 minutes before they were told to leave." Her father told her later he "had to prove to them that the water wasn't going to turn black."[13]

The commissioners finally agreed to provide a road, largely to keep African Americans from using Fort Lauderdale's white beaches. In 1970 the beach was turned over to the state and, in a cruel irony, was named John U. Lloyd State Park after the city's former attorney, who had actually led opposition against allowing African Americans access to the beach. "Dr. Von D. Mizell remains the most significant African-American figure in the life of Fort Lauderdale and Broward County," wrote attorney Don Mizell, his nephew, in 2011. "Despite Dr. Mizell's extraordinary achievements, South Florida lacks a major tribute to his life. That, I believe, can change by re-naming John U. Lloyd State Park, the former "colored beach," in my uncle's honor."[14] As of 2015 the name remained unchanged.

One of Florida's first African American millionaires, Abraham Lewis, would found American Beach, perhaps one of the most famous African American beaches in the country, on Amelia Island just north of Jacksonville, in 1935. The beach was featured in *Sunshine State*, a film made by John Sayles in 2002. Lewis, along with some other men, founded the Afro-American Life Insurance Company in Jacksonville in 1901 to provide African Americans with burial insurance and later medical insurance and pensions. Initially the beach was reserved for company outings, like the Christmas Dance at the Two Spot, but it quickly became a vacation destination for African Americans across the country.[15] According to historian Kevin McCarthy, the company made a statement with the name, calling the "beach American to remind everyone, blacks as well as whites, that the people there were just as American as others in the country."[16]

Marsha Phelts, author of *An American Beach for African Americans*, a history of American Beach, said that when she was growing up in Jacksonville, she would see the signs tacked onto poles near the local grocery stores advertising bus rides to the beach. "About 7 a.m., groups of people would be standing there with their beach blankets . . . their beach bundles," she told a reporter.

The late Mavynne Betsch, the "Beach Lady" who fought heart and soul to save American Beach in the late 1990s, said the beach served a greater purpose. "The Afro provided a world where we didn't have to deal with white folks. My great-grandfather, A. L. Lewis, got us out of the humiliation."[17] There were cottages, clubs, a motel and restaurants, and the place had no shortage of entertainment from the 1940s through the late 1950s, with visits from Zora Neale Hurston, Billy Eckstein, and Cab Calloway. Then Hurricane Dora struck in 1964, followed by the Civil Rights Act of 1964. The effects were almost immediate. One resident told Russ Rymer, author of *American Beach: A Saga of Race, Wealth, and Memory:* "First we had segregation. Then integration. Then disintegration."[18] Marsha Phelts went into more detail:

> Former American Beach vacationers and day-trippers now frolicked on Miami Beach, raced up and down the wide sands at Daytona, wore out the cobblestones of Savannah, and rode high at St. Simons Island. All along the shores of the East Coast, blacks explored areas that had once been off limits. The three-day weekends at American Beach shrank to one day; the Sunday visitors and day-trippers no longer stayed overnight. Loaded buses no longer caused a bottleneck at the crossroads. With so little business most of the restaurants and resort establishments closed.[19]

Facing declining profits, in the late 1980s the Afro-American Insurance Company sold an eighty-three-acre piece of land to the Amelia Island Plantation Company. Until her death in 2005 Mavynne Betsch continued her fight to preserve the beach, which included a sixty-foot-high sand dune she named "NaNa." Her hard work paid off when ten acres were set aside in the Timucuan Ecological and Historic Preserve, a national park. The community of American Beach is still in transition, according to Dr. Carolyn Williams, professor of history at the University of North Florida:

> Some descendants of the original homeowners have kept their properties, but many have sold and moved on. With beachfront and near-beach property at a premium, land values and property taxes have skyrocketed, and many "For Sale" signs have appeared. Looking ahead, will American Beach hold on to its heritage, or will it succumb to the building boom that has transformed most of the island's shoreline?[20]

Long before she rode on a glass bottom boat at Paradise Park, Mary McLeod Bethune, the legendary founder of Bethune-Cookman College in Daytona, began looking for beachfront property in the 1920s to provide "a year round swank winter resort on the sun-drenched Atlantic seaboard of the Gulf Stream state, where Negroes can for the first time have their own beach." *Ebony* magazine reported that

Left to right: Joseph Nathaniel Crooms, Dr. Mary McLeod Bethune, Evangeline Moore, and George Engram stand on what would become Bethune-Volusia Beach. Evangeline Moore is the daughter of Harry T. and Harriette Moore, civil rights activists who were assassinated. Engram and Crooms were co-owners with Dr. Bethune of Bethune-Volusia Beach, Incorporated. By permission of the John G. Riley Archives at Tallahassee Community College. Courtesy of Torrio Osborne.

many "well-to-do Northern Negroes" avoided coming to Florida because of the lack of a "year-round beach," adding that American Beach was only open in the summer. In 1943 Bethune gathered together a group of influential African Americans. Tampa businessman G. W. Rogers headed the project located south of New Smyrna Beach and to be called Bethune-Volusia Beach.[21] Albert Bethune, Mrs. Bethune's grandson, recalled the beginning of the project. "I helped with the development of Bethune and New Smyrna. . . . I would make calls to the wealthy people throughout the country so they could buy shares to the Bethune-Volusia Beach Corporation. [We had] the first black motel on the ocean, the Welricha. Back in those days we had a dance hall and bar that was managed by George Engram Sr."[22]

Plans for building stalled during the war, but in 1948, the company sold 350 lots and Hyder Davie, a night club owner from Miami, built a home. "Biggest bugaboo the corporation has to face in selling sites to outstate Negroes is the fear of prejudice," *Ebony* reported. "Florida's race relations record is not reassuring to the heartiest would-be buyer." In response to this point, N. S. Chaplin, manager of the corporation, said: "Florida is in the South, but it is not Mississippi, and the beach itself is separated from any other section and New Smyrna beach by inlets."[23] According to Joyce Engram, widow of George Engram, one of the original founders, the idea for the beach came about when Bethune took some of her students to the beach at Daytona and were asked to leave. "That didn't sit well with Mrs. Bethune."[24]

Eleanor Roosevelt visited Bethune during this period, writing,

Again, this is segregation, but Mrs. Bethune and her young trustee feel that it is a first step—the bridge between having no recreation for the colored people and the time when all public beaches would be open to all citizens.

I do not like segregation any more than Mrs. Bethune does, but I can see that in the South these steps are almost essential. How must young colored people feel about segregation of the ocean? They see young white people enjoying the natural sport of their age, but for them these areas are forbidden.[25]

Dr. Bethune herself wrote in 1952 that on July 4th, even though the Welricha was "not completed," it was "full to overflowing. The beach swarmed with automobiles of every make and description from every part of the country, from Texas to New York. They brought students and teachers, farmers and laborers, housewives and professional men and women." She envisioned the beach becoming a "great cultural center where great educational conversations can be held, where writers and artists can carry on their creative work."[26]

One of those professional men who visited happened to be a baseball player. Just a couple of years before work on the beach began, Jackie Robinson played his first professional baseball game in Daytona, a town that was chosen purposely for his groundbreaking debut in the minor leagues after whites in Sanford threatened to kill him and Johnny Wright, his Montreal Royals teammate, if they didn't leave town. Daytona was chosen partially because of Bethune's clout in the city. However, even Jackie Robinson wasn't allowed to swim at the "world's most famous beach" in Daytona. He had to drive an hour out of town to swim at Bethune-Volusia beach.[27]

Ironically, because of his grandmother's stature, Albert Bethune said that while growing up he was not exposed to segregation like most black children were, "When I was growing up, I played with the Rockefeller children; I played with the Wright Sewing Machine children, because my grandmother was friends with their parents, so I grew up playing with the wealthy. Where they could go I could go; I could go with them, like the Atlantic Ocean. Black people were not allowed to go there unless they were carrying the white children out there in the water. It was not like that with me because I was with those children. I grew up with those children, John D. Rockefeller Jr. and all that . . . I played with those children.

"Back in those days," he added, "the NAACP was not too interested in desegregating recreational facilities; they were more into the other aspects of desegregation. I know my grandmother was active because I was there to witness it myself." Bethune said he spent time on Daytona Beach. "I was able to go to the races in the early days with my white friends when black people could not go to the races; that's when they had the races on the beach, on the Atlantic Ocean before they made the [track] in Daytona. . . . They had the race on the sand and the hard road on the top, and they would make a circle and go round and round and round."[28]

Still, despite Dr. Bethune's stature in the community, Bethune-Volusia Beach had its own difficulties with racism beyond the obvious.

A woman stands by a Virginia Beach sign that got blown down in a storm in Miami. Virginia Beach was one of the few beaches open to African Americans on Florida's vast coastline. By permission of the State Archives of Florida.

The group did begin building the Welricha Hotel in 1952, but as historian Elaine Smith wrote, "unlike assistance to white developments, both financial institutions and local government discriminated against the Bethune-Volusia enterprise, making its development under black ownership highly problematic. Even so, Dr. Bethune held on until the day she died." The boom that she expected never happened, and many owners had to default on their loans.[29]

In 2002 Charles Cherry, Daytona Beach city commissioner, commented on the demise of the beach. "That was a gathering point for many blacks, but it was 20 miles from Daytona Beach, and the long drive got old real fast." He told a reporter that at the time he remembered thinking, "We're not going to travel 20 miles to go to the beach when I can go one mile from where I live. Our conscience had shifted to the point where our folk wanted to be socially accepted in all areas of American life."[30]

By the 1970s the African American community at Bethune-Volusia beach simply disappeared. During Bethune's day some eight hundred families owned property there, and the corporation was looking to sell nine hundred more lots. By 2003 the number of African Americans who lived on the barrier island had dwindled to eight. African American families who still own property in the area said that integration brought the expected changes, but they weren't prepared for the real estate agents who came in and took advantage of absentee owners, snapping up the land at bargain basement prices and reselling it to whites who suddenly realized the value of the property.[31]

Today the website for Bethune Beach devotes about two sentences to Mary McLeod Bethune's American dream, a beach she envisioned as providing "the opportunity for Negroes to stand on their own feet, in control of a splendid recreational center, open to people of all races and creeds and colors on one of the great waterways of the world."[32]

After Dana Dorsey sold Fisher Island because of rising property taxes, Miami's African American community boated out to Virginia Key, where they established an unofficial "Negro Beach" at a spot called "Bear's Cut." During World War II nearly half a million soldiers descended on Miami Beach to train, and because of the county code forbidding African Americans from swimming in "whites only" areas, Virginia Key was used to train African American soldiers. After the war, in 1945, returning soldiers began demanding equal rights, and a group of men and women led by lawyer Lawson Thomas formed the Negro Service Council and staged a wade-in at a whites only beach north of Virginia Key. "He sent people to get in the water with money in case they got arrested, and sailors joined in," his wife Eugenia Thomas told a reporter in 2004. "The sheriff arrived and told them they knew they weren't supposed to be there." Instead of leading to desegregation or arrests, this wade-in led to talks and compromise, and within a month Virginia Key was listed as a designated "Colored Beach."[33] In 1949 the cabanas and parking area were destroyed in a hurricane, and plans were undertaken to create a beach that mirrored the one at the whites only Crandon Park. When it was completed in 1953 it included many amenities, among them cabanas, picnic areas, a concession stand and restroom, and a carousel and small train—just like the ones at Crandon Park.

When public beaches were desegregated in the 1950s, Virginia Beach was still drawing visitors, although not as many as before. The park was handed over to the city of Miami in 1982; it soon fell into disrepair and was closed. A trust was established in 2001 to restore the park, and it was reopened to the public in 2008. In 2002 when the trust began improvements, Lynette Austin announced that the beach had made it onto the National Register of Historic Places. She remembered going to the beach as a teen. "I remember many [an] evening sneaking out to Virginia Key Beach Park—my parents don't know that—and just simply enjoying a night of dancing at the pavilion." She added that worries about segregation faded into the background against the palm trees and tropical hammocks of Virginia Key: "Why? Because we had the perfect place."[34]

Paradise Found

Nothing like it in the world is what you'll say about Paradise Park, the newest and most unusual recreation area now open in Florida for the use of the colored people of America and the world.

PARADISE PARK BROCHURE

Paradise Park and Silver Springs were divided by an invisible line, and yet, as perfect and lovely as Paradise Park was, there were times when there was no forgetting that it was the daughter of segregation. Bill "Blue" Ray's father, Carl Ray, was one of the owners of Silver Springs and Bill handled publicity for the attraction. "I used to travel the state of Florida handing out Paradise Park brochures," he said in 2005. "The colored people did not consider themselves deprived during trips to the park; as a matter of fact, they had just as much fun as the people at the head of the springs; it seemed like they had more fun." However, he added, "There were differences, and it was wrong."[1]

James Curley Sr., a Vietnam War veteran and the commander of the Veterans of Foreign Wars Brady-Owens Post 7193 in Ocala, re-called a couple of differences, one of which was the way Shorty David-son spoke to the boat captains. "It was the only place that we could go, so we had fun," he said of Paradise Park. "Shorty Davidson was a nice man, but he would call you a 'nigger' in a minute. I remember hearing him saying, 'This is one of my good niggers.'" To emphasize just how segregated the parks were, Curley added, "The only time we would see white people was during the boat ride; they were on their boat and we were on ours."[2]

Nathaniel "Pepper" Lewis began working at Silver Springs as a boat captain in the 1960s, and he too remembered being spoken to in that manner. "As far as whites and blacks being on different sides, that was the way it was; I didn't have feelings about it then," he said, and paused. "You really want to know the truth? You are always going to have prejudice, but the people who worked right along at the spring were like family. Now they may have had their differences, but when it came down to it, they would talk and tease and get along together. On the dock at Silver Springs the guys got along with all the older people working down there. It was pretty nice. And if you got into something—I never got into anything—but some of the guys might have a car wreck, and they were there for you. You didn't go to jail or anything because Ray and Davidson had a way to tell the people something, and then everything was okay.

"People might have had their differences. Old man Davidson might be down there, and he might say, . . . 'These are my niggers. All these are my niggers; don't nobody mess wit' my niggers.' Something like that. And he'd laugh and go on. But at Christmas he'd give everybody silver dollars. That was just his way. He'd take some of the guys fishing.

Pinkney Wood-bury (*back row, left*) with a group of students visiting Paradise Park. Photo by Bruce Mozert. By permission of Bruce Mozert.

That was his way. Every time when I saw him, I'd run. I was really young. I didn't want to see him; I didn't want to hear that word. That's the way I was, 'cause I knew he was going to say it. He didn't care who was around; he was a millionaire. He didn't care. He'd say 'These are my niggers; these are my niggers; these are my niggers.' That was him, a little short guy. But Mr. Davidson in his own way was alright. That was his way, the way he was brought up, but when it came to helping you he would always help you. It was a nice place to work, but he just had that way where he said that word."[3]

Still, as difficult as life could be during the period of Jim Crow segregation, especially for the boat captains who navigated both worlds, Paradise Park was a bright and shining oasis, particularly to the children who visited the park. Despite the irrefutable ugliness of the time, most African American parents managed to shield their children from that humiliation. Mary Carolyn Williams, who later participated in the civil rights protests in Ocala, told the *Star Banner* that having been born in 1948, she grew up with segregation and in her innocence didn't ask questions. "We would go down to the edge of the Springs," she said referring to the glass bottom boat ride from Paradise Park

Boat captain James White takes out a group of tourists who have come to Paradise Park to see Silver Springs. White guided Arlene Francis on a glass bottom boat tour when she staged her television show at Silver Springs in January 1958. By permission of Tina Brito.

to Silver Springs, "and we could see the shops and the glass bottom boats on the other side. I was there with my family, and I didn't need anything else. We had people dancing to music and kids jumpin' in the water. We had fun. Why would we want to go somewhere else?"[4]

Ray and Davidson might have owned Paradise Park, but as former boat driver Leon Cheatom said, "They let Eddie run it. He'd come to them if he had problems or needed something. He made money and he did it on his own; he knew what he was doing. He was a smart businessman."[5] Roosevelt Faison remembered the [Paradise Park] sign Eddie had attached to his car. "He'd pull up outside of Silver Springs by the entrance," he said, hoping to catch any African American tourists who showed up during the days of segregation. "They should've put that car in a museum."[6]

In 1993 when she was ninety years old, Vereen's wife Fannie told a reporter that she worked with her husband until he retired in 1967. "I would help cook. He just loved it."[7] Vereen's sister Mary, who became a school principal, wrote all the advertisements and letters to attract organizations to bring in groups. Eddie Vereen's son Leroy drove the boats part time, and his daughters, Henrietta "Chippie" Cunningham and Vivian Tillman, worked there too. So did his nieces Arizona Vereen-Turner and Catherine Vereen Montgomery and his brother David. Arizona has a photo Leroy Roundtree made of her father David Vereen, standing on the dock at Paradise Park. She said he sold tickets on weekends sometimes. "I worked in the kitchen, in the swim department and in the gift shop. People brought their own swimsuits," said Arizona. "They paid 25 cents for a picnic basket and they would put their clothes in there. We'd give them a number and they'd come back and get their clothes."[8]

Vereen's grandson Reginald Lewis not only posed for the ink blotter advertisement and picked up bottles when he was a child, but he worked at the park when he was a teenager as well, cooking hamburgers, filling in as a lifeguard, and cleaning the grounds. "My granddaddy was very adamant about keeping the place clean. If you went down to meet the boat and there was a piece of paper on the ground, he would remind you to go pick it up on the way back," Lewis told a reporter. "Everything was spotless." He said that whites would pass by the park on their way down river and gaze at the happenings with fascination.[9] "One of my jobs was to keep the white people out. Once this boat

Luresa Lake (*front*) and others lean out of the glass bottom boat *The Richey* for a picture while the guys sit in the boat watching. Photo by Bruce Mozert. By permission of Bruce Mozert. Courtesy of Cynthia Wilson-Graham.

pulled up and I docked it and a white lady got out and said she needed to use the bathroom. I took her up there and went on to do something else. Later we got a call from Silver Springs asking if she was there and the first place we looked was the dance floor, and there she was shaking her rump all over the place."[10]

"We did everything," Catherine told a reporter in 2014. "At that time, we only had so many people employed there. We worked from sunup to sundown, right up until the people left. Then we had all the school groups that would come down from all these different states. So we'd go down at 4 o'clock in the morning, put on the grits and have everything ready for the children when they come in."[11]

Sylvia Jones knows Paradise Park like the back of her hand. She worked in the gift shop, luncheonette kitchen, and bathhouse and on the grounds. She has a drawing she made of the park: the gift shop, bathrooms, snack area, dancing area, pavilion, and the stage where the American Legion held the beauty contests. "There were three hills going up to the main building from the river," she said. "Aunt Fannie loved flowers and she planted petunias that bloomed year-round. There were always beautiful flowers everywhere. And further down the hill, there was the reptile area, the dock where the boats were tied up, the ladder to the diving board, the float. There were picnic areas, a huge barbecue pit, and palm trees and green grass, and that crystal clear water. People played horseshoes. Sounds of fun were everywhere. It was like Paradise.

"Uncle Eddie or Aunt Fannie would pick me, Reginald, and Ron Mc-Fadden up early in the mornings when we weren't in school. We were all cousins. We worked together and played together. We never knew

Lillian Vereen poses with the azaleas at Paradise Park. Photo by Bruce Mozert. By permission of Bruce Mozert. Courtesy of Marion County Black Archives.

Basketball was a popular pastime for young men and women who visited the park. Photo by Bruce Mozert. By permission of Bruce Mozert. Courtesy of Cynthia Wilson-Graham.

what a holiday was; we had to work. We'd have hundreds of buses." She said that even though blacks had access at American Beach in Fernandina, Virginia Key Beach in Miami, and Bethune Beach in Daytona, "there wasn't a place like Paradise Park; people came from New York City and all over the United States; it was the prime attraction for blacks before integration in the South. On holidays it was packed. We had to count buses and cars every day. We had to wipe car and truck bumpers off and put 'Paradise Park, Silver Springs' bumper stickers on them."[12]

Some of those buses were likely Greyhounds. The Greyhound Bus company provided chartered tours to various attractions in Florida in the 1950s. Obviously these tours were segregated. One small announcement in the *St. Petersburg Times* advertised a "'Negro Day' at Cypress Gardens and Boc [sic] Tower."[13] Nat Cherry, a Greyhound employee based in St. Petersburg, was the contact; he also created a tour to Paradise Park after crowds demanded one while returning home

from a previous trip to Bok Tower and Cypress Gardens. Tickets were promptly snapped up, and Cherry advised prospective tourists to pack their baskets so they could enjoy an "old fashioned outdoor picnic" along with the glass bottom boat and jungle cruise rides.[14]

These Florida-based buses weren't the only ones coming through. "I remember one morning we got a call from a man at a gas station near Silver Springs," said Reginald Lewis. "He said that a bus filled with tourists from New York City was there and they were on their way to Miami. They hadn't planned to stop at Paradise Park, but they wanted to come. Papa had us out there at six o'clock in the morning and he cooked breakfast, and we took them on a short excursion down the river, and by 9:00 am they were on the road again." Lewis added that his grandfather met nearly every bus that arrived at the park to greet the visitors and tell them about all the amenities offered.[15]

"Mama would tote the money around in a cigar box on big days like Easter, Labor Day, or the Fourth of July," Sylvia said. "We would put up extra tents on the grounds for snacks and sodas. I started working when I was five. One of my first jobs was posing with a king snake draped around my neck, so white folks could take a picture of a little black girl with a snake around her neck. [Uncle Eddie would] take me down to the head springs; that's where the white folks were. As we got older, we had a big red wagon to play and work with. We had to pick up Nehi soda bottles from the grounds every day. The park was open from sunup to sundown; it never closed. We did everything out there. Our cousin, William Crowell, 'Pretty Boy,' one of the first Silver Springs boat drivers, would pick us up sometimes and we'd get to the park. Sometimes he'd pick up a boat driver and he'd let us off at the head spring, and I'd ride down with the boat driver to dock the boat at Paradise Park. Coming down that river early in the morning when it is quiet and serene is perhaps the most peaceful and beautiful moment on the river. I learned to swim in that river; it was thirty-two feet deep at the diving board. You didn't want to drown. You had to swim about fifteen feet out to the float. Uncle Eddie would make me and Reggie clean up under the float; sometimes we even saw moccasins curled up in the corner. Snails would be on the wooden posts on the lifeguard platform when they were hatching babies. He kept the place spotless."

She said her Uncle Herbert used to tease her about swimming in the water. "Uncle Herbert was the sporty one. He went into the service and lost his arm. He called me 'Gator Bait' my whole life because I learned to swim in that river and there was a gator there that mama said was there when she was a child. I would see it when I was swimming on one side of the river. The gator would lie sunning on the bank on the other side."

Sylvia noted that Ross Allen of the famous Reptile Institute "used to come down to Paradise Park himself to do shows on big days."[16] Allen had several African American assistants who worked alongside him at Paradise Park and at Silver Springs, including J. D. Williams, James Glover, and William Johnson. Reginald Lewis said these men put him to work too. "Mr. Glover kept us busy doing things at Ross Allen's animal compound. Ross Allen had everything down there that was up at the white end. They had an alligator named 'Big George' up at Silver Springs; he was about fifteen feet long. We had 'Old Coochie' who was 19.5 feet long. We had a twenty-foot-long pole out on the dock and I used to put it next to Old Coochie to show people that she was 19.5 feet long." Lewis also remembered capturing a rattlesnake that came into the spring when he was a lifeguard. "I caught him with my bare hands and tried to sell him to Ross Allen, but he didn't want him; he thought I'd hit him with a stick, but I hadn't. People would catch snakes and sell them to him all the time, but sometimes they were bruised and would die shortly after he bought them."[17]

Doris Jacobs-Smith and her sister Johnnye Jacobs said their family went to Paradise Park often. They both remembered the rattlesnakes. "We got a chance to see the deer petting zoo," Doris said, "and you could hear those rattlesnakes ringing, and I mean way before you got there. It was a constant noise." Johnnye agreed."The ringing was so loud because there were so many; they were waiting to be milked."[18] Allen was famous for "milking" the snakes—that is, holding them fang first over a container to collect their venom for scientific purposes—and he frequently made appearances at Paradise Park.

"I would always go to the Reptile Institute," said Samuel Crosby, whose uncle James Glover worked for Ross Allen for more than twenty-six years, beginning around 1949. He retired in 1975. "I never heard Uncle Son say, 'Kill that snake.' He always had respect for them. You don't see that that often. And it was kind of joke with my dad. He would say, 'Sam, black people don't do that,' and I'd say, 'but Uncle Son is doing it.'

"Uncle Son was a very interesting person," he said. "I was just always fascinated by him and those darn snakes and alligators. My cousin Alvin and I were about the same age. Alvin's mother Debra was one of the daughters. We hung out together and I spent a lot of time over at Aunt Ruby's house, that's Ruby Thornton Glover, Uncle Son's wife. Uncle Son would have these crates in the backyard and he would say, 'Don't bother them; there's something in there.' Telling young kids somewhere between fourth and fifth grades not to touch something was like a dare. Alvin and I would go back there and try to peep in to see what was in there. We never got into trouble. We'd see that container and Uncle Son would say there was an alligator or a snake in there."[19]

In the mid-1950s Ross Allen opened a "snake meat cannery" with machinery he bought from George Enns, a rattlesnake canner in Arcadia, Florida. Ben Anderson ran the operation, and James Glover prepared thirty-five to fifty rattlesnakes a day for canning, while preserving their skins and rattles. Both rattlesnake and alligator meat were cooked in Ross Allen's "supreme sauce" before being packed for sale in five-ounce cans.[20] Samuel Crosby said working with diamondback rattlesnakes was not easy. "I knew that was how my uncle got bit one time. They were about to process a snake but he was still alive and bit him." Having a relationship with snakes ran in the family. Crosby said his sister had a pet rattlesnake. "My sister Naomi used to slip from the table; she had to be very young. She'd go up the hill—the family story goes that she was allegedly giving food to a rattlesnake. They told Uncle Son, who told Ross, who told him not to hurt the snake. Finally [Uncle Son] took it away to the Reptile Institute."[21]

Naomi Crosby confirmed the family legend, a venture that could only have taken place in a household where snake handling was the norm. "When I was five years old, I had a rattlesnake I was dealing with," she said. "I would take my food every day, and wrap it in a brown paper bag, and my Aunt Polly would ask me 'Where are you going?' and I would say 'I'm going out,' and I would take the food to the snake." When asked how she managed to befriend a rattlesnake, she said she just saw him in the woods one day. "I kept walking up, and inching up 'til I got close to him and that was it. And I did that every day. I would play with him, and feed him, and he would lick my face." The friendship finally came to an end. "One day he followed me back home, and up under the house. The house was set up off the ground. Some neighbors saw him coming in there behind me and they called my uncle and he came and picked the snake up."[22]

In 1953 Robert Hunter, a reporter for the *Daytona Beach Morning Journal*, wrote a short piece titled "Willie's Philosophy in Snake Pit" about Willie Johnson, who worked at both Silver Springs and Paradise Park as a reptile handler for Ross Allen's Reptile Institute. Hunter described how Willie was working in the snake pit with half a dozen rattlesnakes when one lunged at him. After he explained to the audience that a rattlesnake "won't come after you . . . a rattler only bites in self defense," a woman told him, "I wouldn't go in there for anything. Why aren't you afraid?" Willie told her, "I'm not afraid of snakes. After all, I've lived around humans all my life." Hunter observed that

Of these twelve young men trained at Paradise Park to become lifeguards for Hampton Pool, Robert "Bobby" Thomas, George McCants, and Henry Jones still lived in Ocala at the time of writing. *Left to right*: (*standing*) Robert "Bobby" Thomas, Edward "E. D." Croskey, Dr. L. R. Hampton Jr., Robert "Dukes" Wilson, George McCants, Henry Jones, and Randolph Clark; (*kneeling*) Nathaniel "School Boy" Thomas, Felix "Fley" Cotton Jr., Lucius "Doc Sausage" Tyson, James "J. B." Croskey, and Clarence Coleman. Photo by Bruce Mozert. By permission of the Marion County Black Archives.

"Sometime the truth is spoken in jest," and went on to write what he thought of Willie's philosophy:

> To Willie the deadly reptile is a known quantity and he can safely deal with it. The snake won't cheat him. The snake has no prejudice. Mr. Rattler just as soon will strike a White man as a Negro. . . . We humans take advantage of each other. . . . We love to show our superiority. We're cruel without reason some of the time. I'm not calling anybody a snake in the grass, and this little column isn't going to reform human nature. I just got to thinking about philosopher Willie Johnson's remark in the snake pit.[23]

Hunter's remarks were unusual for the time; what wasn't unusual was the forbearance of the African American men and women, who had to find a way to *live* during segregation. Looking at a photo of his fellow lifeguards who were trained at Paradise Park, Henry Jones explained that many of them also worked at the segregated Hampton pool. They constitute a Who's Who of Ocala: Nathaniel Thomas, Fley Cotton, Doc Tyson, James and Edward Croskey, Clarence Coleman, Bobby Thomas, Dr. L. R. Hampton, Robert Wilson, George McCants, Randolph Clark, and Henry himself. Lifeguard Lucius "Doc Sausage" Tyson and his wife operated Dr. Lowrie's Beach on Lake Weir; Tyson was also a jazz musician who had a hit in the 1950s with "Rag Mop."[24]

"What happened was they had problems," said Jones, referring to the issue of segregated swimming areas and the effect segregation had on finding lifeguards. "They began having swimming at Silver Springs and they were having a problem with integration. Some folks will tell you there wasn't a problem; they rewrite history. It was a problem.

Family members gather on the dock over the Silver River to watch over the children swimming at Paradise Park. Photo by Bruce Mozert. By permission of Bruce Mozert. Courtesy of the Marion County Black Archives.

Because they wouldn't let [black people] swim at Silver Springs, when they got ready to open the swimming pool, they didn't have any licensed guards."[25]

Swimming pool access had been a problem ever since cities began building them in the late nineteenth century. According to Jeff Wiltse, author of *Contested Waters*, "Cities throughout the northern United States built lots of pools in poor, immigrant, working-class-white neighborhoods, but conspicuously avoided building pools in neighborhoods inhabited predominantly by black Americans." He added that during a "pool-building spree in the United States" thousands of huge resort-type pools were built, featuring "grassy lawns, and concrete sundecks, and they attracted literally millions and millions of swimmers." At this time, northern cities began to segregate their pools, and before long, the entire country segregated pools. When African Americans were provided a pool, it was often smaller and lacking the amenities of the whites only pools.[26] In addition to "official segregation," outright violence was used to prevent African Americans from using the white pools. Wiltse told NPR that in 1931 violence broke out when two young men entered the Highland Park Pool in Pittsburgh:

> The police and the city officials allowed, and in some cases encouraged, white swimmers to literally beat black swimmers out of the water, as a means of segregating pools, as a means of intimidating them from trying to access pools. . . . Eventually, whites set up, essentially, sentinel guards at the entrance to the pool, and when black swimmers tried to come in and access them, they were beaten up, sometimes with clubs. They were punched to the ground. They were kicked on the ground. In my book, I have some pictures of black Americans who literally sort of lie still on the ground with bloody heads from being pummeled to the ground, just for trying to access a swimming pool.[27]

Ocala built a thirty-five by fifteen-foot swimming pool for African Americans in June 1956, and as the *Star Banner* reported, "Popularity of the pool was shown immediately when over 400 Negro children signed up for daily swimming classes conducted by trained personnel." The author explained that the pool was "identical in construction to the pool used by white residents of Ocala," except that it was smaller, because "the Negro population is far less than the white population." Inexplicably, the author added that the "Negro auditorium and gymnasium" made up one of the city's "most intensively used structures"; so much for the difference in population size. Until the pool was built, swim lessons took place at Paradise Park. Edward Croskey explained to the paper that beaches and lakes were great for swimming, but "if you are going to teach swimming the pool is the only place to do it."[28]

Henry Jones and the other lifeguards were trained at Paradise Park by the legendary underwater swimmer Newt Perry, who later founded the Weeki Wachee Springs mermaid attraction. "Newt Perry had taught himself how to swim and he was with the Red Cross doing certifications. He taught us how to life guard. If you've ever seen a picture of Newt—he was huge. Now here we were all of us sixteen or seventeen years old, and we had to take him out of the water in a fireman's carry. He'd dive down to the bottom, and we'd have to dive in after him and get him, bring him to the top, put him in the fireman hold, and bring him out of the water. On land he'd put sand in his mouth and we'd reach in with our fingers and get the sand out and give him respiration. That was graduation day. We also had to swim a distance with a concrete block held straight out. You haven't hurt in the middle of your back till you've just used your legs to swim, carrying the dead weight of a concrete block. I can't say everybody made it." Henry added that as famous as Newt Perry was, he didn't take a picture with the young men he trained, "because it wasn't politically good."[29]

The Rev. Dr. Tommy Brooks Jr., pastor of New St. John Missionary Baptist Church in Ocala, agreed that simply learning how to swim was difficult during segregation. Before Hampton pool was built, African Americans only had a few spots on rivers and lakes to swim. "I can remember asking everyone to carry me across the river," he said of swimming at Paradise Park. "We swam with the moccasins and gators. As long as the gators were full, we didn't worry about them. Paradise Park was the only place to swim unless you wanted to go down to Lowrie Beach. I remember when the school bus would bring people to Paradise Park every Saturday so they could learn how to swim. A few years later Hampton Pool was built, and the young men would have to pass the Red Cross Exam in order to become a lifeguard. The test was hard to pass," said Brooks, who at age fifteen became one of the

Robert "Bobby" Thomas, one of the first Red Cross–trained lifeguards at Paradise Park, holds up a picture of himself. He scored the highest on the swimming examination. Photo by Cynthia Wilson-Graham. By permission of Cynthia Wilson-Graham.

youngest lifeguards working at the pool. "I don't even think I was of legal age."[30]

One of the people who didn't attempt to swim with the alligators at Paradise Park was the late Mayo Faison Sr., a senior deacon at Ramah Missionary Baptist Church in Belleview. Faison married his wife Viola on Christmas Eve in 1931, and they were married for an incredible seventy-three and a half years, only separated by their passing in 2005 and 2006, one year and five days apart. He had a long history with his church as well; his family was among the original members, a group of ex-slaves who founded the church in 1892. The church celebrated its 120th anniversary in 2012.[31]

Faison knew what he liked and didn't like at Paradise Park. "I liked looking at the big fish through the bottom of the boat. I didn't swim, so I rode the boat. I remember they would dump you into the lake until you learned how to swim. I remember this one time a fellow was swimming in the river and the alligator got behind him. So he swam across the river and walked back. Swimming wasn't for me."[32]

Swimming was something former Paradise Park beauty queen Gloria Johnson Pasteur said she wanted to do but couldn't. "I could not swim, but I always wanted to swim. Back in that time girls were so full of life and everything. They had a big float in the water and I wanted to get to that float. Well, the boys would help me get to the float, but then I could not get back, unless they came to get me." She said Paradise Park was dear to her because her family spent time together there picnicking. "We used to go there, like on Labor Day and on Sundays, and those were some of the good times that I had with my father, because he would be with us, and we would take blankets and my mom would 'fix' stuff and we'd be sitting up under the trees with him, and it was just good, 'cause he was kind of sickly; he had asthma. I would see my friends at Paradise Park, and everybody would basically be doing the same things with their families. . . . [My father, Oscar Johnson, was] a good man. His people came from Cotton Plant, Florida. He would take us out to Paradise Park. He drove a taxi. They called him Peanut because he and his daddy sold peanuts, and that was another way my aunt, Alma Johnson, got to go to college."

The patrons of Paradise Park used the same river and rode the same glass bottom boats as the patrons of Silver Springs, but they never crossed the invisible line that separated the parks. The boats would

Among the 1954 contestants in the Miss Paradise Park Contest sponsored by the American Legion were Gloria Johnson Pasteur (*left*) and Earlene Archie (*third from left*). Photo by Bruce Mozert. By permission of Bruce Mozert. Courtesy of Cynthia Wilson-Graham.

Boat captain David Faison poses for a picture after returning from taking visitors for a ride down the Silver River. After fifty-nine years at the springs, he still enjoys visitors and the history of the springs. Photo by Cynthia Wilson-Graham. By permission of Cynthia Wilson-Graham.

pass each other on the river: African Americans on one side, whites on the other, although Gloria remembered that sometimes the bus drivers would come to Paradise Park. "There were a few white people there but not that many. I saw the bus drivers, maybe in the pavilion part. There were maybe two white people, but I never saw many white people during that time. Some people just looked white."[33]

David Faison began working at Silver Springs in 1956 and at this writing was still working there. "Roosevelt was here; I was working in a saw mill. I had one kid when I was here—my only son Durban—came in 1956. My wife Gert was pregnant with my daughter Audrey in '57. I was running a boat then. I came into the dock, and old Raymond was working the dock and he said, 'Old man, a lady came here in a white Buick with your wife in it and said she is mighty sick,' and I said 'Yes, I know she is.' Boy, I had a '51 Chevy and I got into that car and drove straight to the hospital—the baby done come. I said 'Niecy what do we have?' and she said, 'A baby girl.' I said, 'Good.'"

Faison described how Paradise Park would send for a boat when there was a crowd. "Miller Davis used to run it down there, and Tim Howard worked down there. They'd carry a boat down there and see if people wanted to ride. If they got more [people] than they could take, they'd call up here and tell Miss Martin, the ticket lady, 'We need somebody to go to Paradise Park."[34]

"If it got slow at Silver Springs, we had to go down and make picture frames for the souvenir photos," said Nathaniel Lewis, referring to the photos Bruce Mozert made of the white tourists. "That's how they kept us busy. They didn't want you sitting around." When captains were called to run boats at Paradise Park, he said, they found an appreciative audience. "The blacks enjoyed it more—it was exciting for them—and they tipped better. I'll put it that way; they really tipped good. You might come out there and get ten or fifteen dollars. You take a load of whites, you might only get two or three dollars—they wouldn't tip. That was the difference."[35]

Henry Jones said he drove one of the boats for Paradise Park even though he was too young to have a license, but he did learn how to "crack the peanut. That's parking the boat without hitting the sides." Before he finessed parking the boat, he had to learn how to drive one. "I'd duck down and hide in the boat, so they couldn't see who was driving. My uncle would call up to Silver Springs to send a boat down. Sometimes they were tied up because they were busy and Leroy Vereen would drive the boat, and after a while Nathaniel "Schoolboy" Thomas and I drove. He promoted Schoolboy to work as a boat guide. So Schoolboy went up to Silver Springs. In the summer my uncle would drive around and advertise a lot and when he went out of town, the boat guys would take me out. There were two chutes and they'd let me park their boats. I could drive good and after a while when Uncle Eddie came home one time, I told him I can drive a boat. He said, 'I'm gonna check you out,' and he took me out there and sat down in the boat and I took him across the river and showed him how I could navigate around the Catfish Hotel and gave him my spiel. And I asked him if I could drive. He said, 'You're too young to get a license,' but he let me drive sometimes. They still had the wood boats and about three they'd be off. So I'd take my wood boat up there and get that fiberglass boat. I could make two trips because it was faster. We'd get tips. I'd have a coin in my hand and there was a little fire extinguisher up there and I'd put my hand up there. And all of sudden the river was clear; the water was boiling up out of the spring and I was coming in. . . . I'd drop that dime or that nickel on that glass and it would bounce around. If it was a church group I might drop a silver dollar, depending on the group. And they didn't know where that money came from . . . that's how you made your money."

Henry recalled an ugly incident he had with segregation and the electric boats. "I had an elderly couple on the boat. They charged the boats all night, but I could tell it was getting weak, so I pulled in where the white boat captains park," he said, referring to the white jungle cruise captains. "I was going to switch boats and this guy said, 'You can't park the boat here,' and I tied it up, and said, 'If you touch that boat, we're both gonna drown today.' Back there where they wanted me to go, the water was too low for those old people to get out. I had no choice. All the boats [belonged to] Silver Springs. Silver Springs owned everything.

"Remember, Paradise Park owned nothing. The jungle cruise boat would come down if they could get free; the glass bottom boats were sort of on call. The drivers wouldn't stay long, because they couldn't make a lot of money. My uncle made money off the concessions and the swimming and he'd go advertise. I'd drive with him. We'd drive all day long up to schools in Georgia and Alabama; he'd give out brochures."[36]

Some of the schools that took advantage of the opportunity to expose children to the educational aspects of Paradise Park were from nearby communities. Whitfield Jenkins, community activist and former president of the Marion County NAACP, grew up in Bethlehem, a small town about ten miles from Ocala. "We had a two-room schoolhouse," he said. "Silver Springs and Paradise Park usually came up when teachers planned a special event. The schools didn't have access to county school buses, and Paradise Park was about twenty miles from school, but sometimes they would plan for a whole year and some students would go to Paradise Park for a field trip. That's how I found out about it. I think when I was in the fifth or sixth grade I came to Paradise Park on one of those trips. I had never seen a glass bottom boat where you could look down and see the fish; it was like going into outer space."[37]

The first brochures made for Paradise Park touted the amenities:

[It] is regarded by many prominent civic, business and religious leaders throughout the nation as the finest thing of its kind ever built for members of their race. At Paradise Park, for the first time, the colored

Left: The outside of a Paradise Park brochure featuring the glass bottom boat and a photo of Luresa Lake. By permission of Cynthia Wilson-Graham.

Below: The inside of a Paradise Park brochure advertising the amenities of the attraction. By permission of Cynthia Wilson-Graham.

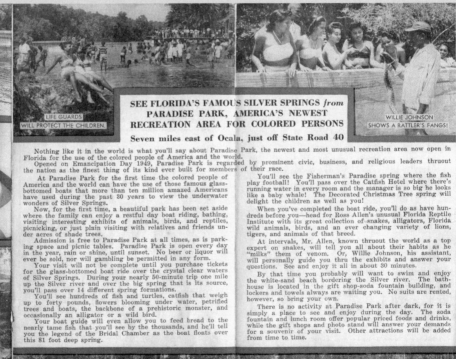

people of America and the world can have the exclusive use of those famous glass bottomed boats that more than ten million amazed Americans have used during the past 30 years to view the underwater wonders of Silver Springs.[38]

The brochure featured images closely resembling those on the Silver Springs brochures, except that the people enjoying the glass bottom boat, the girls petting the deer, the bathing beauties splashing through the water, the beauty resting on a palm tree, and the children playing on the beach were all African American. The photos were similar because they were made by official photographer Bruce Mozert, who pioneered underwater photography at Silver Springs in the 1930s. The late Lottie Donaldson, then a physical education teacher at Howard Academy, posed underwater holding a "See Paradise Park" sign.

"They wouldn't allow anyone else to photograph at Paradise Park," said Bruce. "Mr. Ray controlled it. I was the only one allowed and I took hundreds of photographs. It was a beautiful place, and it was well done and in good taste. And they had all the benefits at that time, going on the glass bottom boat, the jungle cruise. They had a wonderful park for picnicking and for the scouts. Every year they had a large beauty contest and people came from all over to enter. So I happened to get a lot of pictures of all the activities. . . . I even had a photographic darkroom where I developed photos I made of people on the

Bruce Mozert, the legendary photographer who worked at Silver Springs, was the only professional photographer allowed to photograph patrons of Paradise Park. Photo by Cynthia Wilson-Graham. By permission of Cynthia Wilson-Graham.

Lottie Donaldson was the only African American woman Bruce Mozert could convince to pose for one of his famous underwater photographs. Here she displays an ad for Paradise Park. Photo by Bruce Mozert. By permission of Bruce Mozert. Courtesy of Cynthia Wilson-Graham.

glass bottom boats. I had an African American boy, one of Reverend Pinkston's sons, who worked the darkroom and an African American girl who sold the pictures, just like we did at Silver Springs. Everything we did up there, we did at Paradise Park."[39]

Luresa Lake was one of Mozert's models whose image appeared on the brochures and on postcards. "I had no dreams that I was beautiful or whatever, but everybody thought I was perfect, so when the photographer came to take pictures at Paradise Park, they pushed me out front. He said I had the right size and everything. I was just married. We went over to Silver Springs, and there were four or five of us." Lake has a postcard featuring her reclining on a palm tree that appears to angle out over the river. "We were not really over the water, but when he took the picture, it appeared to be over the water, and I just thought I was somebody. You couldn't tell me anything. I'm posing for a picture like this! And when this came out, oh my goodness—Ocala recognized me as somebody. That made me happy."[40]

Although Mozert was the primary photographer at Paradise Park, the attraction was a magnet for other photographers as well, from the amateur to the professional. The late Leroy "Tree" Roundtree was a former military police officer who owned a photography studio on

Luresa Lake, aged eighty-four, admires a picture of herself that was featured on brochures and postcards of Paradise Park. Photo by Cynthia Wilson-Graham. By permission of Cynthia Wilson-Graham.

Broadway Street in Ocala. "I was a self-trained photographer; I traveled around the state of Florida taking pictures. I think that Bruce Mozert gave me additional training when I was taking pictures at Paradise Park, but it's been so long ago, so I don't remember if it was Mozert or someone else at the park. I remember driving from Miami with my 'rolling mobile trailer' attached to my car. I built the trailer to run my business. I would go out to different places and set up my photo business and make about fifty to a hundred dollars a day. People would bring their children from all over the place for me to take pictures. Mozert was already established in taking pictures at Paradise Park, but sometimes I would still photograph other individuals at the park. I can remember taking pictures of people on the boat before they left for a boat ride and when they returned, I would have the pictures all made up." He said he sold the pictures at six for a dollar.

The boardwalk was a popular place to take pictures at Paradise Park. Photo by Bruce Mozert. By permission of Bruce Mozert. Courtesy of Cynthia Wilson-Graham.

The commander of American Legion Post 306 awards Martha Thompson her gift as she becomes Miss Paradise Park in 1958. Photo by Bruce Mozert. By permission of Bruce Mozert. Courtesy of the Marion County Black Archives.

Unfortunately, nearly all his pictures of people in the park were destroyed in a home fire in 2000.[41]

The most photographed events at Paradise Park were the annual Labor Day beauty contests established by Florida's Negro American Legion Posts in 1949. The American Legion of the Eleventh District of Florida in Ocala headed up the first event and Vice-Commander L. C. Rackard said he expected 7,500 people to attend the festivities, where at least twenty contestants from Jacksonville, Sanford, Marianna, Tallahassee, Clearwater, and various other cities would compete for a diamond ring. Rackard said the contestants would be also photographed and filmed for newsreels "made for Negro theaters throughout the nation."[42] The very first Miss Paradise Park was Mildred Jones; Alfronia Johnson came in second and Arzella Bryant was third.

Alfronia Johnson made it into the contest after being selected at a preliminary beauty contest at the Roxie Theater. Later two of her daughters, Gloria Johnson Pasteur and Carrie Johnson Parker-Warren, entered the contests and placed as well. "I was a runner up in the beauty contest," said Gloria. "I was in the ninth or tenth grade, and I had a picture. . . . I was holding a lamp" (shown earlier in this chapter). She said people came from all over the state for the beauty contests, some from as far as Pensacola, along with all the out of state visitors. "Sometimes we would get angry because we could not find a spot to sit, because there were so many people. Going to Paradise Park was a freedom that I enjoyed, and a closeness of family. So many people don't have that, didn't have that at that time, but I did, because my father was there."[43]

Carrie Johnson Parker-Warren remembered her crowning as well. "It was either eleventh or twelfth grade when my mother announced to the family that I was chosen by Mr. Rackard and his group to represent Ocala in the Paradise Park Beauty Contest." She said she couldn't remember being critiqued or even seen, but because her mother and sister had placed, she thought "maybe it was just a 'Johnson Girl Thing.' Mrs. Lottie Donaldson, my physical education teacher, and Mr. Nelson, my art teacher, were the ones who taught me to walk, smile and deliver as a participant. I can remember the lessons and instructions were conducted at Mrs. Donaldson's home, in her living room. Mrs. Beulah Jackson was my hair stylist and makeup artist. At the contest, she was a bit surprised that I had changed my hair (as school girls often did). My shoes were purchased at Malevers's in downtown Ocala, of course on my Aunt Alma's account. At this point, I am not sure where my mother purchased my one piece black and white swimsuit. I was dressed for a grand pageant and of course, I won First Place, Miss Paradise Park, with a twenty-five-dollar check as the winning prize. Most people of color in Ocala at that time were in attendance. This was a day of celebrations and crownings; Ocala did not always win but expected to do so. These memories will remain with me and my family forever."[44]

LaRone Taylor Davis also remembered being asked to enter the contest when she was seventeen and still a student at Howard High. "This event was one of the highlights of my early life. A small group of the local members of the post approached me to ask me to compete in

Alfronia Morgan Johnson was one of the first contestants in the Miss Paradise Park contest in 1949. Photo by Bruce Mozert. By permission of Johnson family.

Carrie Johnson Parker-Warren (*front*) was the winner of the ninth annual beauty contest held at Paradise Park at Silver Springs on Labor Day; more than five thousand people attended. Photo by Bruce Mozert. By permission of Bruce Mozert. Courtesy of the Marion County Black Archives.

the contest." She too received training from Mrs. Donaldson and hair styling by Mrs. Jackson, "a noted beautician in Ocala. The competition was intense because it was the culminating summer extravaganza for the African American community. The winner was seen not only as a beauty queen but as a young lady who excelled educationally and would represent the community in a positive way. I received a check for twenty-five dollars and was featured in several black newspapers. I was not recognized by the *Ocala Star Banner*. I never entered any other contest but went on to complete my education, earning a master's degree in education. I married the late Mr. Edward D. Davis and I am the mother of two children."[45]

These days she is also the secretary of the Orange County NAACP. Her husband was also an activist; he was the principal of Howard Academy when a group of teachers, including Harry Moore, gathered to organize a protest against unequal teacher salaries. Edward Davis was considered the "firebrand" of the group.[46] He was inducted into the Florida Civil Rights Hall of Fame along with former governor Reubin Askew in 2015.

Silver Springs boat captain Virginia Ferguson said the beauty contest was her favorite event at Paradise Park. "Everybody looked forward to that; everybody celebrated at Paradise Park. The girls were busy before trying to get enough money to get their outfits, their bathing suits. It was a real beauty contest. The girls came from all over the state. It was like going to a Superbowl party. I know one girl who participated; her name was Martha and her father was a Pentecostal preacher, and he didn't know she'd entered. There was hell on Tucker Hill after that. And believe it—now she's a preacher."[47]

The American Legion post often used the event to raise money for good causes, like Eccleston's Crippled Children's hospital. Some of the winners over the years include Sallye Chavers of Ocala, 1955; Rosalyn Dew, 1956; Martha Thompson, 1958; Harriet Wyatt of Daytona, 1959; and LaRone Taylor, 1960. Annie Lois Anthony of Tampa won the title in 1962, the first year that the Legion added a talent show to the mix. Jackie Robinson's mother, Mallie Robinson, was on hand for this pageant.[48] Jackie Robinson returned to the state many times as a civil rights activist, and in 1964 he arrived in "racially troubled" Ocala, as a reporter described the city, to speak at a civil rights rally organized by the Ocala NAACP.[49]

On Easter Monday, one year after Paradise Park opened, the attraction hosted Bethune-Cookman Day. Henry Jones recalled seeing the famous educator. "Dr. Bethune came down; she was wearing a white suit, a skirt and jacket. And she stood next to the jukebox and gave a speech. Then it wasn't popular to say "My little black boys and black girls . . . ' Back then you couldn't call somebody black; they'd fight. She said it, and it was alright. I saw her in person—that was the only time I saw her. When she came to Ocala she stayed with the Crumps."[50]

Edgar Samuel said he remembered seeing Dr. Bethune as well. "I

Contestants in the 1960 Paradise Park Labor Day Beauty Contest. Crowned the winner was LaRone Taylor of Ocala (*second from left*), entered by American Legion Post 210. Second place went to Nora Hazel Sheffield of Tallahassee, with Jonquill Flowers and Shirley Ann Taylor tied for third. Photo courtesy of Marion County Black History Archives.

remember [her] and five of her friends coming over to Paradise Park to ride the boat at Silver Springs. Buck Ray said to Sammie Cheatom that none of the white drivers wanted to drive the boat. Dr. Bethune and her guests rode the boat with white guests."[51]

Dr. Bethune, who wrote a regular column for the *Chicago Defender*, wrote about her visit to the park: "On this past Easter Monday, Bethune-Cookman Day was observed at Paradise Park, Silver Springs, Florida—one of the state's most beautiful recreation centers. It was a glorious day for me." She noted the "generous gesture of the owners of

FIRST ANNUAL

Bethune-Cookman College DAY

AT THE

Silver Springs Paradise Park

Seven Miles East Of Ocala, Florida, Just Off Highway 40

STATE COMMITTEE PLANS BCC DAY

| PARADISE PARK | BETHUNE-COOKMAN COLLEGE |
| Silver Springs, Fla. | Daytona Beach, Fla. |

the park, Messrs. Ray and Davidson, in contributing all the proceeds of the day's activities to the treasury of our appreciation." At the end of her article she seemed to make a reference to segregation at the Springs:

> And I thought of all those who call me "friend"—all over America. Silver Springs was a challenge to all of us to use every opportunity for advancement; to realize the importance of our franchise; to register and vote in every nook and corner of this country until our civil rights are fully realized.[52]

Dr. Bethune's grandson Albert Bethune, interviewed at age ninety-three, remembered driving himself and his grandmother to Paradise Park. "I've been driving a car since I was fifteen years old. When I graduated from high school in 1939, my family gave me a Plymouth Convertible car as my gift; it was paid for out of the family business, Bethune Mortuary, one of the leading mortuary businesses in middle Florida. So ever since then I have been driving, and as I got older I continued to drive; when she needed to go to St. Petersburg, Tampa and other places, I used to do the driving for her."

"I went to Paradise Park with my friends many times, but I did take her there a few times. Silver Springs was sixty miles from Daytona to Ocala; the drive was just like going downtown back in those days. People were having parties and picnics and things like that, so I followed the crowd. Paradise Park was alright, but it wasn't up on a par with the white part of Silver Springs. It was not like the main Silver Springs presentation. My grandmother didn't care too much for Paradise Park because it was segregated. That's why she went along with Dr. Hampton. The Hamptons were one of the popular families in Ocala. She was a medical doctor, and he was a dentist. They were close friends with

Many visitors enjoyed playing horseshoes at Paradise Park. Photo by Bruce Mozert. By permission of Bruce Mozert.

my grandmother and wanted to see Silver Springs desegregated, just as she did."[53]

Easter Sunday became the official opening for the summer season at Paradise Park. "On Easter Sunday there was always a countywide sunrise service," said Sylvia Jones. All the churches would come, have a service, and do baptisms. Service started about 5:30 a.m., and the spirit was truly present in that environment. Aunt Fannie would cook grits, fish, and hushpuppies and we'd help. On the Friday and Saturday prior to that we'd boil thousands of eggs and color them, and we'd have a big Easter egg hunt on the Monday after Easter with sections for older kids, young kids, and adults. It was a big deal every year and a lot of work."[54]

The "Town Talk" columnist reported in 1963 that Paradise Park "was scattered with Easter eggs Monday, bringing hundreds of local youngsters to the annual hunt. A huge nest of gaily colored eggs was arranged especially for the tiny tots." A group of high school students from Spaulding High School in Lamar, South Carolina, was on hand for the festivities.[55]

As Sylvia said, all the churches would do mass baptisms at the river. Timothy Green, a former master gardener at Silver Springs, was also

Baptisms at Paradise Park were held at sunrise services on Sunday mornings before the park opened. Photo by Bruce Mozert. By permission of Bruce Mozert. Courtesy of the Marion County Black Archives.

Remembering Paradise Park

Christmas was celebrated at Paradise Park with the arrival of area preachers and Santa Claus (Timothy Howard). Reverend O. V. Pinkston is the first preacher on the left. Photo by Bruce Mozert. By permission of Bruce Mozert. Courtesy of the Marion County Black Archives.

deacon at St. Mary's Missionary Baptist Church, one of the many local churches that baptized its members in the Silver River every Easter Sunday. In June 2000, when he was eighty-five, he was on hand for a historic baptism: Silver Springs allowed St. Mary's Church to baptize LaKecia Douglas in the headwaters, the first time a church member was baptized in the Silver River since the late 1960s. Green told a reporter that he couldn't remember how many baptisms he had attended at Paradise Park, but he knew that every Easter Sunday for years about a dozen people waded into the cold water to be baptized. "I think I attended every one of them."[56]

The boat captains tell a story about the time a glass bottom boat filled with white tourists approached the area where a baptism was about to take place. One of the tourists piped up and said, "I ain't never seen a Negro baptism before!" and the boat captain calmly wheeled the boat around, heading back up the river, replying, "And you ain't going to see one today."

Churches from surrounding towns would also bring members of their congregations over. Journalist Bill Maxwell said his grandfather, who was a pastor in Crescent City, took people over to Paradise Park to be baptized. "They had used Lake Stella almost exclusively," he said. "Then he got together with some other pastors and they decided to do group baptisms and they would pack into cars and head over there. It was quite an event. They would bring food and have dinner on the grounds, so it turned into a whole day affair. I think I went to two of those. I wasn't religious at all but I did like to be around all the people and the good food."[57]

Virginia Ferguson explained another reason churches would come out. "They didn't have pools in the churches, so they would use the Silver River. When I was baptized again about six years ago," she said, "I was baptized at the head of the river. At that particular time the alligators were nesting and the general manager required us to have life guards, but it was still beautiful."[58]

By 1953 Paradise Park was drawing 150,000 guests a year, so many that a reporter from *Ebony* did a piece, describing the park as the "newest and largest recreational attraction for Negroes in the South . . . a mecca for thousands of holiday celebrants." One large photo accompanying the article featured Nathaniel Thomas standing on a log underwater. Another featured children gathered around a man sitting on top of an alligator.[59] Ida Lee Donaldson Berry got into big trouble for posing for one of Bruce Mozert's photos that was to appear in the magazine. The photographer arranged a group of six young women around a billboard proclaiming "Turn Here for Paradise Park!" Because they were wearing swimsuits the image caught the attention of a local minister, who alerted Berry's father to a postcard made from the image, and he was not pleased. Berry told a reporter that he punished her, saying "No young lady exposes her body parts like that." Still, she said, "I didn't see anything wrong with it."[60]

Lottie Donaldson, a dance teacher at Howard High School, and Nathaniel "School Boy" Thomas, one of the first lifeguards at Paradise Park, are featured in one of the few underwater pictures made there. Photo by Bruce Mozert. By permission of Bruce Mozert. Courtesy of Cynthia Wilson-Graham.

The late Freddie Lee Perkins explained why people flocked to Paradise Park. "The first few years the park opened there was nothing near Ocala until Club Bali opened. After Paradise opened, people would come from Orlando, Jacksonville, Daytona, and Palatka because there was no place for blacks to go to. If you lived in Daytona, they did not allow you on the beach, because of the white people. I remember going to the park just to be around other people. I almost gave my mother a heart attack, because I would dive off the diving board and she didn't know I could swim. I learned to swim at the head of the springs, where the petrified log was, back in the forties. We used to go out there to shine shoes; we would put our bathing suits in the bottom of our shoe shine box. The alligators were not that bad . . . you didn't have to worry about them, because the river had plenty of fishes, so they had enough to eat."[61]

The day after Christmas was always a big draw. Looking at a photo of children gathering around Santa, Brenda Vereen explained how Christmas meant oranges. "During orange season—and this is orange country, with lots of groves down in Weirsdale—that would be the

A contortionist performs for the crowds at Paradise Park. Photo by Bruce Mozert. By permission of Bruce Mozert.

The Christmas holiday season was a time when many families gathered at Paradise Park. Often the park staff would distribute oranges to the families. Photo by Bruce Mozert. By permission of Bruce Mozert. Courtesy of the Marion County Black Archives.

biggest thing they could get for so many people. You'd go out to get your Christmas boxes and we were real proud of our Christmas boxes. And you'd see Santa Claus. At that time I believed it. We saw he was real."[62]

Narvella Haynes also remembered going to Paradise Park to see Santa. "I was six, seven, eight, starting out. We played games, played in the sand, put our feet in the water. At Christmas time they had all

ROSS ALLEN'S
REPTILE INSTITUTE
SILVER SPRINGS
FLORIDA.

3008

those oranges out there and you'd see Santa. Everything was joyous; you didn't have much during that time. I lived in the rural area so when I went to Paradise Park it was a big outing with my parents and my uncles and aunts. It was family oriented. Everybody on the block would pack up and go. Looking back, there is so much to miss; the buses would come from everywhere. That's how I learned about different cities in Florida: Gainesville, Tallahassee, Miami—it was exciting to see all those people, more at Paradise Park than in the city."[63]

The late Frank Pinkston, whom historian Thelma Parker of Ocala described as the "Black Liberator of Marion County" for his leadership in the civil rights movement, risked his life to organize sit-ins at local businesses to bring on desegregation. Still, even in the midst of his important and dangerous civil rights work, he took the time at Christmas to enjoy Paradise Park with his family (see chapter 2 for a 1950s photograph of him and his daughter with Santa Claus).

Carol Croskey also had a photo of herself with Santa Claus. "I do remember years ago having a picture of Santa Claus on one of the glass bottom boats waving to us kids on shore. Of course the glass bottom boats fascinated me. At first I was afraid to ride them because I just knew the glass was going to break. I wasn't a good swimmer. Six-year-olds have lots of fears. As I got older and knew better, the boat ride was a breeze. I was fascinated with part of the tour at the 'catfish motel.'" Croskey remembered a variation on the football game the captains got the fish to play. "I loved it when the driver would stop the boat for the baseball game. He would take bread and roll it into a ball, drop it into the water and call the 'game.' I really believed the fish were playing, especially when he said the fish ran the bases. All of the fish made homeruns. My saddest memory was when the park closed because segregation was no longer the norm. I was sad because Silver Springs was so big and overwhelming and didn't have the same warmth as Paradise Park."[64]

Ocala also had a Christmas parade that included "everything from an alligator to Santa Claus." The Howard and Fessenden academies and Paradise Park always had floats in the parade. Henry Jones said when he traveled to schools in other states with his uncle, they would participate in homecoming parades too. "We'd go to parades in these towns, if they had a homecoming parade. Paradise Park had a float with glass around it and snakes. We had a cousin, Cynthia Vereen,

Facing page: Cynthia Vereen, granddaughter of Paradise Park manager Eddie Vereen, was not afraid of snakes. Here she holds up a snake as long as she is tall at Ross Allen's Reptile Institute at Silver Springs. By permission of Eric Larson, proprietor of Cardcow.com.

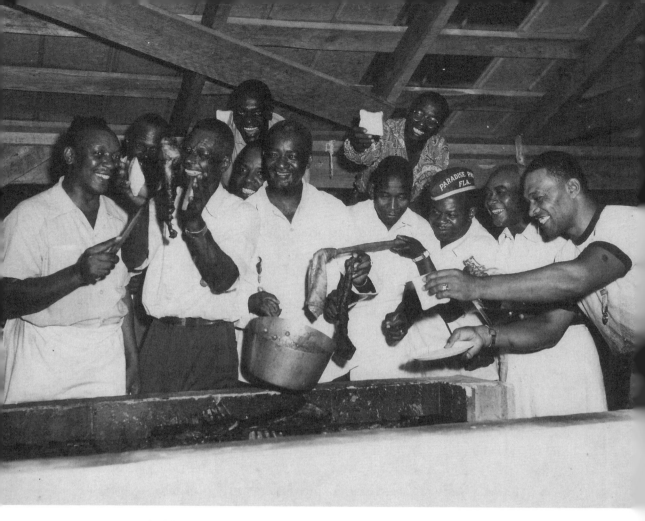

A group of men have fun in one of the pavilions at Paradise Park, apparently engaged in a cooking contest. Photo by Bruce Mozert. By permission of Bruce Mozert. Courtesy of the Marion County Black Archives.

who'd go in there with the snakes and pick them up. I'd never go in there. The float was a glass bottom boat."[65]

"Cynthia would be in that glass container with the snake around her neck," said Arizona Vereen-Turner, "and I'd be in my bathing suit standing on top of the boat. I had a little shape back then."[66] Samuel Crosby remembered his reptile-handling uncle, James Glover, participating in parades on the West Side of Ocala as well. "I used to always wonder why he was the last one in the parade on the West Side and I finally figured out that it was because of snakes. He had snakes in the car and people didn't want to march behind the car with snakes. It was a convertible. He used non-poisonous snakes like boa constrictors or indigo snakes. Either Louis or Betty would be in the car with snakes around their necks."[67]

Oscar Collins began working at Silver Springs the same year that Paradise Park closed, making a sort of imperfect circle of his life on the river; he had gone to Paradise Park as a child, unable to visit Silver Springs, like all the other boat captains who worked there during segregation. "That's where all the churches had their picnics," he said. "They also had the Future Farmers of America convention at Paradise Park. That was a school thing. I did the Easter egg hunt on Monday with my siblings. They'd hide the eggs on Easter Monday because there was no school. They had swimming, and a place where you could play horseshoes."

He also recalled Eddie Vereen's big "See Paradise Park" sign on the side of a motel on Broadway. "I think they could have kept both parks and let people decide where they wanted to go," he said of the closing. "White people went to Paradise Park too; we just couldn't come up here. It was a nice park. It was history. . . . I just think people should've been able to go wherever they wanted."[68]

That sentiment is shared by many people who spent time with their families at Paradise Park, including Dorsey Miller. "They could have done some upgrading and just made [Paradise Park and Silver Springs] all one, a real integration," he said, "and if we wanted to go to the park we could have gone to the park, or if we wanted to go the main site, Silver Springs, we could have gone to the main site; but they didn't. They obliterated our site and wiped out our history and our culture."[69]

Who obliterated Paradise Park—literally knocking down the pavilion, luncheonette, and picnic tables and dismantling the dock—isn't exactly clear, but the likely culprit was ABC. "Who bulldozed it?" said Roosevelt Faison. "I don't really know, but after ABC bought it, they cut this Fort King waterway through there and it goes right through Paradise Park and I guess they might have gotten rid of it during that time."[70] The Fort King Waterway was part of a project launched by ABC to help Silver Springs compete with Disney World; they established an animal preserve along the waterway. As Tom Cavanaugh, part of the team that bought Silver Springs from ABC, told a reporter in the 1990s, "As you go down Fort King waterway, sitting on the right hand side, you see the giraffes with big oak trees. That's where Paradise Park was."[71]

When Ray and Davidson sold the attraction to ABC in 1962 the *Ocala Star-Banner* reported that the sale included huge tracts of land along each side of the Silver River, all the way down to the Ocklawaha, in addition to the "internationally known boat ride . . . the Aquatorium, the

Joseph Wheeler II and his family at Paradise Park in 1957, photographed by his mother, Fannie Delaney-Wheeler. Left to right: (*back row*) his father, Joseph Wheeler, his grandfather Frank Delaney, and Buddy Mitchell; (*front*) Joseph R. Wheeler II and his brother Edward L. Wheeler. By permission of Joseph Wheeler II. Courtesy of Alonzo Hardy.

Ross Allen Reptile Institute, the Seminole Indian Village, the Bartlett Deer Ranch, the Prince of Peace Memorial and Calvacadia."[72] There was no mention of Paradise Park. Just the year before, Paradise Park reported that the "largest crowd of the summer season" was on hand to celebrate its thirteenth Labor Day beauty contest, with Jackie Robinson's mother in attendance. There was no mention of ABC. That was how it had always been. In 1959 when the Public Relations Association voted Ray and Davidson into the Hall of Fame of Outstanding Floridians "for the skill with which they fashioned a Florida phenomenon into one of the nation's most visited attractions," with 1.5 million visitors a year, it is doubtful whether they counted the families picnicking and swimming at Paradise Park or the young men and women dancing next to the jukebox.[73]

When Silver Springs was completely rebuilt after a devastating 1955 fire, in a "modern style Florida motif a la Frank Lloyd Wright," complete with souvenir and coffee shops, a restaurant, and covered walkways to protect people on rainy days, it didn't make a ripple at Paradise Park.[74] When the Aquatorium—a large air-conditioned underwater theatre—was built in 1962 to "provide visitors with more time to leisurely view the underwater world" and give them "additional time and improved facilities for making underwater pictures," the people at Paradise Park did not raise their cameras to their eyes.[75]

When Howard Hughes staged an underwater premier of his film *Underwater!* the Paradise Park visitors weren't on hand to see Jane Russell, although when *Jupiter's Darling* was being filmed, boat driver Willie Marsh did get to make a few tips off the white tourists who wanted a look at Esther Williams. "I liked Esther Williams," he said. "I could make money off of her. She had a double, and people would say, 'Just take me over there where I can take a picture of Esther Williams,' and I would, and they'd give me three dollars, five dollars. Yes, that's Esther Williams. And they'd yell 'Esther.' And she'd wave back to them."[76]

A Day at Paradise Park, 1957

Alice Robinson Rozier

The Robinson family exemplifies how people used and loved the park during the years when gracious and pleasant places for African American families to enjoy swimming and picnics were hard to find. Interviewed for this book in 2014, Alice Robinson Rozier offered a guided tour of the suite of family photographs shown here, all taken at Paradise Park on the same day in 1957.

My mother, Mrs. Willie Mae Robinson, truly enjoyed going to Paradise Park during the holidays and any day we could. She loved theme parks, amusement parks, and going to the beaches in Daytona, St. Petersburg, and Fort Lauderdale. My mother always thought that any time was a good time for a picnic. You do not see my father in the pictures because he was in the United States Air Force. He retired in 1970 after thirty years of service. After integration, we would also go to Cypress Gardens and Rainbow Springs. My mother lived in Ocala all her life and recently passed at the age of ninety-five years and ten months.

I can still remember the excitement in the air at Paradise Park. We would ride the boat from Paradise Park to Silver Springs to see the legendary Ross Allen who handled the rattlesnakes. There were beauty pageants

Carolyn Mosby Adams stands in the center of the field at Paradise Park during an outing. By permission of Alice Robinson Rozier.

Deloris Robinson Clark and her little sister Alice Robinson Rozier visit Paradise Park on a hot summer day. By Permission of Alice Robinson Rozier.

and games at Paradise Park. The children would explore the park, catching minnows at the water's edge with cups and just running through the park. The alligators did not seem so threatening during that time. I do not remember having any fear of them when we saw them sunning on land.

When my family looked at the photos with us all dressed up, we laughed. Those were the times we dressed up for special occasions at Paradise Park. There were times we also dressed down for picnics and would swim in the lake. We knew the Vereen family because we all attended the same church. My sister Deloris's best friend was a Vereen. I now know that the Vereen family played a major role in the management of the park.

The photos show me, my mother, Mrs. Willie Mae Robinson, and my sisters, Deloris Robinson Clark, Celestine Robinson Johnson, and Patricia Robinson. The young man is my brother, Eddie Robinson Jr. We called him "Brother"; and the other young lady is my cousin, Carolyn Mosby Adams. These pictures were taken in 1957. My sister Deloris, standing near the Paradise Park sign with my younger sister Patricia, was home for the holidays. She was in college at Florida A&M University. Deloris is retired from being director of nursing at a hospital in Clarksdale, Mississippi. She left Ocala in 1970, returned to Florida in 1994, and currently resides in Orlando.

Left: Deloris Robinson Clark and her little sister Patricia Robinson pose in front of the Paradise Park sign during a visit to the springs with the family. By permission of Alice Robinson Rozier.

Right: Eddie Robinson Jr., Deloris Robinson Clark, and Celestine Robinson Johnson enjoy a day at Paradise Park. By permission of Alice Robinson Rozier.

Patricia is a retired elementary education teacher in the Marion County school system and always lived in Ocala. I am a retired university administrator who worked for several universities: Florida A&M University, Florida State University, and Florida Atlantic University. I now live in Orlando. My sister Patricia and I both attended undergraduate school at Bethune-Cookman College in Daytona Beach. My graduate work is from the University of Florida and Florida International University. Patricia graduated from Forest High School in Ocala in 1973 and I graduated from Ocala High School, 1970.

The picture with my two sisters and brother is such a classic. My brother is on the left with a hat on, my sister Deloris is in the middle, and my sister Celestine is on the right. My brother was very popular in high school and was well known in Ocala. He was a businessman and passed in 1997. My sister Celestine attended Hampton Community College. She was a housewife and lived in several states and out of the country before moving back to Ocala in 1986. Her husband also retired from the United States Air Force after thirty years of service. My sisters and brother in this picture all graduated from Howard High School in Ocala: Deloris in 1956, Eddie Jr. in 1958, and Celestine in 1961.

I just love the picture with my mother standing with us kneeling at her feet. My sister Celestine is seated on the left, I am in the middle, and my cousin Carolyn Mosby Adams is seated on the right. You see my sister Patricia wandering off in the background on the right. Carolyn also graduated from Howard High School. She graduated from Gibbs Community College in St. Petersburg and the University of Florida. After graduating from UF she moved to Fort Lauderdale. She moved back to Ocala several years ago and is a retired psychiatric nurse currently working to open the Estella Byrd Whitman Health Clinic, named after my grandmother. Then you see Carolyn again, standing alone in front of the grand ballroom area. You see all the classic cars behind her. These are truly memories to embrace. These were good times for my family. I was in high school when Paradise Park completely closed. We then started a tradition of going to Silver Springs and we went there often, also. We would ride the jungle cruise and glass bottom boats and attend all the animal shows. It wasn't until my father became ill in the late 1990s that we stopped going as often.

Paradise Park will always be in our hearts and minds.

Willie Mae Robinson loved going to Paradise Park with her children. Her husband was away in the air force. At her feet (*left to right*) are her children Celestine and Alice and her niece Carolyn Mosby Adams, and daughter Patricia is off in the background. By permission of Alice Robinson Rozier.

10

The Beginning of the End

Young Negro voices from the white, clapboard church were singing:
"If you can't find me at the city jail and you don't see me anywhere /
Come over to the county jail I'll be singing there." Up the highway
toward town 11 young Negroes—eight boys and three girls—sat in
Marion County jail cells and said they'll stay there.

DON PRIDE, "NAACP UNITS PICKET TOGETHER"

In September 1963, just one year after ABC bought Silver Springs and
the surrounding properties, Ocala would find itself, courtesy of the
White Citizen's Group, accused of launching a "legal, physical, and
psychological" harassment campaign to make "Ocala the toughest
city in the U.S. to desegregate." The charge was made by the Florida
Advisory Council to the U.S. Civil Rights Commission. Robert Saunders, field secretary of the NAACP, told a reporter Ocala was in a
"police state situation," because of the "deterioration of the lines of
communication"—a situation not altogether surprising, given that
Ocala was Florida governor Farris Bryant's hometown.[1] When he ran
for governor in 1956 Bryant told a crowd, "I'm for segregation. . . . In
the homes of Negroes we find different intellectual levels and moral
and sanitary standards."[2]

Saunders's observation came after a series of incidents that included mass arrests of demonstrators protesting the arrest of Zev
Aelony of the Committee on Racial Equality; "juvenile demonstrators"
being charged with delinquency; and gun shots being fired into Dr.
L. R. Hampton's house, both "two to three years ago" and "once last
July." Hampton told police that the latest shots had been fired into his
daughter Gwendolyn's bedroom, and "two pellets pierced a toy rabbit

L. C. Stevenson, who helped start the Hunting and Fishing Club in the 1960s to protect civil rights activists, poses here with his rifle. Photo by Cynthia Wilson-Graham. By permission of Cynthia Wilson-Graham.

lying on the little girl's bed." She wasn't home at the time. What made that incident even more horrifying was that Hampton's brother Leonard, known as "Shy," was married to Annie Rosalea Moore, a teacher at Howard Academy. Her parents, Harry and Harriette Moore, were the first two civil rights activists killed in Florida when their house was bombed on Christmas night in 1951.[3]

A group of local African American men got together during this period of violence and formed what they called the Hunting and Fishing Club, as the "protection arm" for those in the civil rights movement, according to Mary Carolyn Williams. "They were always at our weekly mass meetings and made sure that we were all safe inside Covenant Missionary Baptist Church. Their vigilance continued as we left the area, en route to our homes. They also made sure that our leaders were protected. The need for their services became more evident when men in a truck shot into the bedroom window of the daughter and youngest child of Dr. and Mrs. L. R. Hampton Jr."[4]

The Hunting and Fishing Club owed its origin to "the shrewd minds of the NAACP," according Whitfield Jenkins, former president of the Marion County NAACP. Not only had Dr. Hampton's house had been shot at; Frank Pinkston was under constant threats against his life. "During that period you could have been in some difficulty if you were caught bearing arms and did not have a good reason," said Jenkins. "The formation of the Hunting and Fishing Club was the legal way for blacks to bear arms to protect Pinkston and other members of the NAACP."[5] According to the *Star Banner*, the founding members of the club were "L. C. Stevenson, Moses Menchan, Ivory Dukes, Willie Reed, Johnnie Dyous, Oscar Donaldson, W. C. Grigler, Joseph Reese, Gilbert Mack and Frank Nelson."[6]

L. C. Stevenson recalled that the club organized in the garage of a house on Fifth Street and began protecting the mass meetings, the Youth Council, and Reverend Pinkston himself. "We would go over to Covenant Church and sit outside and watch people coming in and out, and after that we would escort Reverend Pinkston home and park down in 'Nebo City' way out in the woods." He said members of the club would not carry weapons with them because they were wary of being stopped and charged by the police, so they would leave the weapons in the woods at Pinkston's home. "We would stay out there till the break of dawn, then we would leave and come on back to get ready for work." He said such diligence was necessary. "I strongly believed that Reverend Pinkston's house was going to be bombed like Mr. Harry Moore's house. That was my reason for dedicating my services to the Hunting and Fishing Club."[7]

Moses Menchan described how members of the club protected Pinkston's home. "We had 50 feet of lights," he said. "You could walk anywhere in the area and mash a button and those lights would come on at each corner of the house. We had cans hanging on a wire so if anybody walked through the woods at night and we didn't know they were there they would hit those cans and we would hear them. We also had our own dugouts. We were trying to protect ourselves, the Pinkstons and everybody else." That meant climbing into trees, said William "Wimpy" Freeman, the group's youngest recruit. "That was my perch. I could see further down the road from each vantage point. I could see cars approaching from each direction from a distance."[8]

According to Dorsey Miller, civil rights activists had been quietly

Reverend Frank Pinkston helped lead the civil rights movement in Richmond, Virginia, when he was a student at Virginia Union. He came home to Ocala in the 1960s and continued leading the movement even though his life was threatened many times. AP photo. By permission of Lu Vickers.

busy in Ocala for several years prior to the very visible movement that emerged in 1963. "Very little was said about it," he said. "During the school year of 1960–61, we had a club called the Esquires at Howard High School. There were about twenty-two of us in that group. One day, in September of 1960, we decided that we were going to desegregate some of the lunch counters downtown. As we were marching down Broadway, some of the parents came and pulled their children out of the group. We had on red ties, white shirts, and blue pants, and we went to McCrory's Five and Dime Store and sat at the whites-only lunch counter. The manager closed down the lunch counter and we left and headed over to the public library. We fanned out all over the library and sat at different tables. We were allowed to stay and read books and nothing was said. So after that, that library was integrated. We did not go back; we just made a statement. We were told that we were not going to graduate because of what we had done, but naturally we all did. That was the first attempt to desegregate facilities in Marion County, which was three years before the 1963 movement, and the movement continued in 1970–71."[9]

In 1960 Frank Pinkston was a student at Virginia Union in Richmond, Virginia, where he helped lead the sit-in movement. Along with other student leaders, he had been trained how to demonstrate by Martin Luther King Jr., and after a meeting in February 1960 Pinkston helped lead a march from Virginia Union to Woolworth's lunch counter, where the manager refused to serve the students, then shut down the lunch counter. The group's next target was Thalhimers, an upscale department store. Thirty-four students went into the store, some heading into the Richmond room upstairs while the rest made their way to the lunch counter on the first floor. They were all arrested, including Pinkston, and the group gained the name the "Richmond 34."[10]

David Rackard, who was a student at Clark College in Atlanta, said the student protest movement had not made it to Ocala at that time. "Dorsey Miller and I were demonstrating in Atlanta, but nothing was going on in Ocala. When we came home for the summer we started talking about demonstrating in Ocala. They used to have a grocery store called 'White Davis' and a grocery store called 'Colored Davis.' Colored Davis was across from Covenant Missionary Baptist Church." Colored Davis was where Robert Houck, the president of the Ocala NAACP, had an office.[11] Both buildings would play a role in the movement.

Like Rackard, Dorsey Miller was also a student in Atlanta, but Miller was at Morehouse. He too said there was no NAACP Youth Council in Marion County at that stage. But one day he was contacted by Charles Washington, who at the time was a student at Hampton Junior College in Ocala. Washington told Miller that the Student Non-Violent Coordinating Committee (SNCC) was organizing sit-ins in Dunnellon and suggested they get a group together to do the same in Ocala. Miller, Washington, and Rackard then met with Robert Houck of the NAACP in his office at the Colored Davis store. Houck told them that the NAACP itself only had seven members, and they didn't have the resources to start a youth council. Miller said, "We were very disappointed, but we said okay. As we were leaving his office, I said, 'I'll tell you guys what; let's go over to Covenant and talk with Rev. O. V. Pinkston, and maybe he will let us use their dining hall for a meeting. Pinkston immediately said yes. Rev. O. V. Pinkston is the unsung hero of the Civil Rights Movement in Ocala." L. C. Stephenson, former head of the NAACP, echoed Miller's sentiments: "He was the only one

The Reverend O. V. Pinkston and his wife, Amelia Mae Jones Pinkston, were active in the civil rights movement in Ocala. Reverend Pinkston opened the doors of Covenant Missionary Baptist Church to mass meetings. Photo by permission of Amelia "Ann" Pinkston.

who would let his son have mass meetings at his church. No other church in town would accept him because of fear."

That Friday they had their first meeting, and almost two hundred students showed up. Miller said he presided over the meeting and was nominated president but declined in favor of Charles Washington, since the venture had been Washington's idea; Miller also wasn't sure if he would be around all summer. "We talked with Rev. Pinkston about allowing us to use the church and giving us some office space," said Miller. "He allowed us to have offices there during the week; we used the Sunday school classrooms as offices for what we called the NAACP Youth Council."

The next phase of the youth council took place when the group approached Frank Pinkston, the elder minister's son, because they needed to return to college. "We talked with Frank and told him we needed his help," said Miller. "He agreed, and that was the beginning of the Ocala Movement."[12]

Frank Pinkston was the Reverend Clarence Cotton's cousin. Cotton said that from 1960 to 1963, at the time desegregation finally arrived in Marion County, he had just begun working in the school system. "That was when the inklings of desegregation were coming around."

Cotton was drafted into the service, and after serving "nine months and six days" he came home. During that time Pinkston had begun organizing the sit-ins. "When I came back, I got involved. My cousin and I had attended school at Virginia Union University, and if anyone followed the history, it was clear that the sit-ins were tied to Frank coming home. We worked hard at that at Richmond before Frank and I came back home. When we came here with those ideas, it was the same. We had been to the sit-ins and gone to jail in Richmond; we'd done all that already, so we came here with those ideas. Richmond was the capital of the Confederacy."[13]

"We were tired of being treated as second-class citizens," Pinkston's sister Ann told a reporter in 2006. "The day was over for going to the back door, going to separate water fountains, going to the back of the bus or riding the bus from one end of the county all the way over to the other end of the county literally to go to school, versus going to a school that was near you."[14]

The NAACP Youth Council, supported by Pinkston—who by then was president of the Ocala chapter of NAACP—began demonstrating around Ocala. Miller remembered going into the Ocala Coffee Shop on the Courthouse Square, where they planned to enter one at a time. "I was the first to go in, but I will never forget there was this white policeman. He was well known in the black community, because he was extremely hostile to blacks. His last name was Cash. That was the first time I was happy to see Cash, because when I walked into the Ocala Coffee Shop, they immediately locked the door to keep anybody else from coming in, so I was the only black person in there. I remember one of the customers saying, 'Give me a hot cup of coffee, and make it as hot as you can.' I imagined they were going to try to throw the coffee on me, but Cash came in and said, 'Dorsey, get out of here.' I was only too happy to leave."

The Youth Council targeted the lunch counter at McCrory's as well as the Marion Hotel and Liggett Drug Store. Miller said he led a group of about fifteen students to Liggett's, where they sat on the stools surrounded by adults, like Thelma Parker, who came along to make sure they weren't attacked. "The manager of the store came out and asked if I could come to his office. I asked Bob Rice to come with me; Bob Rice was a legendary football player at Howard High School."

The manager made a phone call, then turned to Miller and told him if they were to "leave and not cause any disruption, the lunchroom counter would be desegregated. Liggett's was the first place in Marion County to desegregate."[15] Bitting's Drug Store wasn't as conciliatory, Miller said. "Rather than desegregate, he took his lunch counters out." H. E. Bitting, who owned the store with his brother, was City Council president and acting mayor of Ocala at the time.[16]

"We held mass meetings at New Covenant Church here that were standing room only," Sylvia Jones told the *Ocala Star Banner*. "We sang songs like 'We Shall Overcome' and called for a boycott of the segregated stores downtown until grass grew on the sidewalks. Ocala had a strong civil rights movement. The NAACP was involved, and it was youth fueled with lots of energy. I helped make signs and organize the demonstrations." She was one of the first African American students to integrate Ocala High School. "We had daily confrontations but stuck together. When Dr. King was assassinated, the names of the black students were called out and we were asked to report to the auditorium. We were told, 'We don't want any trouble,'" she told a reporter. Sylvester Jones, her grandfather, was afraid for her because she was outspoken. "My family was so concerned my grandfather kept driving by the school with a hidden shotgun. My grandfather was very polite and almost submissive. He thought we were too rebellious."[17]

Guy Musleh, the attorney who had accompanied Thurgood Marshall to lunch when he was in Ocala for the Groveland Case, was the county prosecutor at the time. He said he would "prosecute every person who violates the law" and added that he didn't "understand the reasoning behind the incidents of deliberately trying to provoke disorder in Marion County." Other whites seemed confused by the sit-ins as well: "We thought we had the best racial relations anywhere, because we have been helping the Negroes for years to get better educational and recreational facilities."[18]

But that was not how local African Americans saw it. "We wanted to do away with segregation," said the Reverend O. V. Pinkston years later. "It was inferior. They tried to make it seem like we had everything but the quality for us was inferior," he said, referring to the auditoriums, the schools, the swimming pools.[19] His wife was involved in the movement as well. "This is the governor's hometown; we wanted things done smoothly," said Amelia Pinkston in 1963 at the height of the protests. Her friend added, "But they're acting like it's something they don't have to bother with, like it will go away if you put enough Negroes in jail. But these young Negroes are not like we were 50 years ago. It's not going to go away."[20] And indeed it didn't. Frank Pinkston was arrested a few days after the protests downtown for overseeing a group whose placards "failed to identify their leadership." As Pinkston was released, he told a group, "We'll fill the jails today."[21]

Meanwhile the nation's eyes were not only on Ocala but also on St. Augustine, where extreme violence was being acted out. During a Ku Klux Klan rally in September 1963, two months after the Birmingham church bombing, Dr. Robert Hayling and three other men were brutally attacked with "chairs, axe handles, sledge hammers, and ball bats," barely escaping with their lives.[22] Although Hayling wasn't the first person to agitate for civil rights in America's oldest city, the dentist's selfless and forceful nature—and his newcomer status—pushed him to the forefront of the movement. He wasn't beholden to anyone in town and simply wasn't afraid to act—which nearly cost him his life and did cost him his livelihood. In 2014 he was inducted into Florida's Civil Rights Hall of Fame, recognized officially as the "Father of the St. Augustine Movement" as well as the father of the legislation that would come with this movement.[23] The St. Augustine Movement got its start in March 1960 when Congress signed off on a resolution to establish a commission to organize a celebration for the city's 400th anniversary in 1965. No African Americans were named to join the group. The intervening years were filled with bombings, Klan rallies, shootings, and other forms of terrorism. In July 1963 a group of students were arrested at a lunch counter, including four teenagers who ended up jailed for a month before being sent to reform schools where they spent five months. Governor Farris Bryant finally released the St. Augustine Four after the story caught the nation's attention.

Dr. Hayling contacted Martin Luther King Jr. and the Southern Christian Leadership Conference in March 1964 seeking assistance for the increasingly violent situation in St. Augustine. King, working feverishly to pass the Civil Rights Act, recognized that St. Augustine would be a mighty catalyst in that effort. In June 1964 King arrived in St. Augustine, where he told the press he would bring in a "non-violent army of whites and Negroes" if necessary. The next day the cottage where he was staying on Anastasia Island was blasted with bullets. By June 11 he was arrested on the steps of the Monson Motor

Civil rights protesters (*right*) have a stand-off in the Atlantic Ocean as they stage one of many wade-ins in St. Augustine, the nation's oldest city. By permission of the State Archives of Florida.

Lodge—the only time he was arrested in Florida. Meanwhile, protestors did wade-in after wade-in on St. Augustine Beach, risking their lives each time they stepped into the Atlantic Ocean.[24]

A week after King's arrest, protestors held a "pray-in" at the hotel, and the following day a group of seven protesters, both black and white, jumped into the pool. James Brock, the manager, was famously photographed dumping into the water a two-gallon jug of muriatic acid, which is used to clean pools, to force the swimmers out. It didn't matter that a two-gallon jug of muriatic acid was essentially harmless. The sheer vehemence of James Brock screaming, "I'm cleaning the pool!" was acid enough.[25] On July 2 President Lyndon Johnson signed the Civil Rights Act of 1964, which outlawed segregation in public facilities and outlawed job discrimination. After the Civil Rights Act of 1964 passed, more Marion county restaurants were integrated, but it would take years, indeed decades, for the situation to improve. Ocala was still being sued in federal court in the late 1990s for failing to "meet its court ordered desegregation quota."[26]

Eddie Vereen (*left*) and his assistant, Doretha Smith, with Phillip "Big Hat" Jiles, a disc jockey from up north. By permission of Reginald Lewis.

Whitfield Jenkins said he was one of the first black teachers to work in a white school in 1967–68. "That was the year the federal government gave the Marion County school district a chance to integrate voluntarily. There were black teachers who taught in white schools and white teachers who taught in black schools, and I can tell you that it was an experience that was unique because it was teachers—adults—who wouldn't come in the lounge when I took my lunch break. They would not come into the lounge and eat if I was there. And there was a white teacher, a science teacher there, Mrs. Moss, who was so affected by it that she came to me and asked me to come and have lunch in her classroom so I wouldn't have to experience that."[27]

In 1969 Paradise Park was quietly closed. No committees were formed; no one sought out members of the black community to discuss alternatives. The last announcement for the summer season was a soulless note that appeared in the *Star Banner* on May 20, 1968, exactly nineteen years to the day after it opened: "Paradise Park at Silver

Springs opened its season Saturday according to an announcement from Silver Springs Corp. The Park will be open on Saturdays and Sundays, and all holidays during the Summer."[28] Manager Eddie Vereen had retired on February 1, 1967, and according to Reginald Lewis, Doretha Smith and Catherine Vereen Montgomery took over managing the park; but its days were numbered.[29]

Gone were the loving pronouncements that had appeared in the column "Town Talk," such as this one from 1963: "Paradise Park, popular resort, is now an aura of beauty as numerous blooming flowers and shrubbery pervade the area."[30] Gone too were the choirs and the preachers who led the sunrise services, gone were the beauty queens, and Santa Claus, and the children who searched for eggs the Vereen family had prepared and hidden.

Riley Williams followed his cousins, the Faison brothers, to Silver Springs in 1959 and retired around 2003. "I went down to Paradise to drive the boats," he said. "It was good, all those years. I never regret one day of going down there; even after I started working on the grounds, I still liked it. The tourists were about the same at both places. There were twenty-one boats out there; you'd go down the river, come right back up to the head of the spring and unload and go down again. They'd call up there from Paradise and say 'Could you send us a boat down here?' Sometimes guys would volunteer to go down there. Guys would want to go down there and make the run. They'd take the same trip."

He remembers the moment when he realized that the boats would no longer have to make the same trip from separate docks. "Well, before they closed Paradise Park, they didn't want the whites and the blacks riding the same boat and afterward, they didn't want to integrate up at Silver Springs—they didn't want to do that. I remember one day I was standing up there [on the dock] and Mark Dupree, that was the head man, told Randall Hughes—I was standing right there, and there were black people getting on the boat, but he didn't want to put them there—and Dupree told him, 'Put 'em on.' And I got it right then. He told him; and all those years that were segregated ended when he told him, 'Put 'em on.'"[31]

Roosevelt Faison likewise recalled Dupree supporting integration. "After the civil rights bill passed, Mark Dupree was the general manager. Paradise Park was closed. People would show up here and he

A view of Paradise Park from the parking area. Photo by Bruce Mozert. Permission of Bruce Mozert.

would come downstairs to make sure the guys on the docks would put people on the boats. And that's what he did. When they walked up, the white guys loading the boats would look up, and he'd give them the nod. He was following the letter of the law. It went both ways. If he didn't do it, he'd get the company in trouble, and if he did do it there was the chance he'd meet opposition from the local people who were opposed to integration. I remember him saying, 'If they come here, they're going to be taken care of here; they're going to ride.'" But, Faison added, "They didn't want to just get out and advertise because there was a lot of tension and he wanted that to ease off as much as possible. So blacks were taken care of when they came, but [the park owners] weren't reaching out, trying to get them in. They weren't advertising down on Broadway."[32]

And West Broadway, already weakened, would be decimated around this time, when I-75 was built. The seeds for this destruction were perhaps inadvertently sown in 1962, when Ocala's leaders worked "behind the scenes with Gov. Farris Bryant's office" seeking to have an exchange placed on I-75 at SR 40. They argued that the exchange "was vital to the future of Silver Springs as a tourist attraction."[33] Ten years later, city planners decided to create a four-lane overpass to make funneling tourists into Silver Springs even easier. But even that overpass would prove to be of little help to Silver Springs as the effects of Disney World's arrival rippled outward. Like many other attractions, Silver Springs simply could not compete with Disney, and its glory days ended as well.

Former boat driver Nathaniel Lewis described how desegregation did in both Paradise Park and West Broadway: "It was right to integrate but it took away a lot from the black community. [Beforehand], you had all black stores up and down Broadway, clothes, grocery stores, cleaners, pool rooms, all kind of things, little joints where you eat, little taverns. You can't go buy a loaf of bread from a black store now."[34]

When African Americans were fighting for their civil rights, said Clarence Cotton, "the closing of Paradise Park wasn't something that we wanted, but we didn't have a choice. They decided after desegregation to close. If we had a choice, it would probably still be open today. I am sure business fell off at Paradise Park, so they just abandoned it. I'll be honest; I've worked here in Ocala for several years in the school system and then I left and came back, and Paradise Park held so many memories for me that I went down the little country road that took you to where the gate was locked, and I climbed over the fence to go there. It was all overgrown."[35] Years after it closed, the *Star Banner* ran a brief article on the history of Silver Springs, closing with this telling description: "[Paradise Park] continued operations paralleling those at Silver Springs until federal desegregation guidelines resulted in the closing of the Black park and expanding the other in the past decade."[36]

"Silver Springs was not ours," said Dorsey Miller, "and then they had taken what I felt was ours, Paradise Park, away from us, and that left some bitterness in me. They could have maintained Paradise Park, and let that be integrated too. See, it was not integration that occurred

filmed at
PARADISE PARK
SILVER SPRINGS
FLORIDA

A group of young women pose next to the azaleas on the grounds of Paradise Park. Photo by Bruce Mozert. By permission of Bruce Mozert. Courtesy of Marion County Black Archives.

for us; it was desegregation and assimilation. That's what it was; we never experienced any integration. Integration is when you bring two things together and meld them into one. We never had that. It was the same with everything else, the schools and everything. They took away our culture, our history, and tried to assimilate us into theirs. They could have done some upgrading and just made Paradise Park and Silver Springs all one, a real integration, and if we wanted to go to Paradise Park we could have gone to the park, or if we wanted to go the main site, we could have gone to the main site, but they didn't. They obliterated our site and wiped out our history and our culture."[37]

Part of that culture involved family gatherings, picnics, and music. "Paradise Park was our roots," said Brenda Vereen. "Silver Springs is nice, but it was nothing like Paradise Park. We could just get out there

By 2014 Roosevelt Faison had been a boat captain at Silver Springs for fifty-eight years. In 2014 the St. Johns River Water Management District recognized his long history on the river by organizing a project to capture his observations of the changes he has seen on the river over more than half a century. Photo by Cynthia Wilson-Graham. By permission of Cynthia Wilson-Graham.

and have a good ole time like we wanted to. I miss it because it was like family. I don't care where you came from—when you got there, you were family. We had picnics, dancing; we don't do that anymore. At Silver Springs we couldn't have picnics; we couldn't dance. I don't even know—did they even have a dance hall over there? That's what drew the people to Paradise Park, the jukebox. Mr. Vereen organized that; he knew what the community liked. It just goes back to our roots. We always liked music and food. I would have liked to see a part of Paradise Park stay open after integration."[38]

Roosevelt Faison felt that the closing of Paradise Park "put us all together as one in the place of being divided. It's got its place in history, but I was glad to see it go because it meant we weren't divided anymore, and black people could come up here and see what we had, which was more than what we had down there. I don't know why they didn't include it in the history."

He said Bob Gallagher, who managed the park in the late 1990s and early 2000s, talked about having the boat drivers include the story of Paradise Park in their spiels. But there were pitfalls. "When you start talking about race relations, that's a real touchy situation," Faison said. "You've got to handle that really carefully. If you get out there with a lot of different people and you get one captain to handle it wrong, to say the wrong word in the wrong place, you could bring in a whole lot of trouble for the company. I told him at the time that it was alright but you're going to have to really be careful with what you say, and who says it and how you word it and all that. He finally forgot about it, and it's that way until today. You could embarrass black people and you could embarrass white people. It is history, but there are a lot of things we've done in the course of history that we don't really want to face up to anymore. The state might include that history, but the state is different than a private corporation, because the state is governed by all of the people, and if they don't handle it right then the federal government can get involved, so it's different from a private corporation. It's definitely part of history; it's ugly but it's there. It didn't go away just because all the signs were removed. It left scars."[39]

Indeed, the state now owns Silver Springs, and whether it will honor the memory of Paradise Park in a meaningful way remains to be seen. In 2013 a group of people representing state agencies and water management districts traveled down the river with Faison, who by then had worked at Silver Springs for fifty-seven years. Among the officials was Ed Lowe, chief scientist with the St. Johns River Water Management District. "Roosevelt went through the standard tour speech and then stopped and asked us, 'What are you going to do about all the algae in the spring? How are you going to fix it?'" Lowe said. "I stayed behind afterwards and engaged him in a conversation. This man is a keen observer. He has an affinity for the springs. He appreciates the beauty of Silver Springs and has seen the changes that have occurred and he's really concerned." Lowe decided to capture Faison's recollections of Silver Springs in a documentary film. "Roosevelt has an intuitive understanding of how an ecosystem works. He understood that with the decline of the grass and fish populations there would be a decline in bird species. . . . I felt it was a real privilege to meet this man and I appreciate his willingness to share what he has observed over the years."[40]

One can only hope that state officials will feel the same way about documenting the cultural history of Paradise Park and the legacy of Eddie Leroy Vereen. Many of those interviewed for this book were disturbed at the lack of acknowledgment that the park had even existed. Ignoring it "was sad to me because that was part of my life," Ocala native Narvella Haynes told a reporter in 2006. "To think it was not even important enough to mention. For some reason, depending on who writes the history, certain parts are not recorded."[41]

Samuel Crosby explained the effect that his connection with Paradise Park had on his life. He adopted a "live and let live" philosophy: "I got teased a lot, because if kids found a snake in the community they would call me. I didn't want to hurt him. I wanted to catch him and let him go. Even when I went hunting when I got older, if I ran

Bathing beauties of the season at Paradise Park include Susie Long and Patricia Bright (*second and third from right*). Photo by Bruce Mozert. By permission of Bruce Mozert. Courtesy of Cynthia Wilson-Graham.

The Beginning of the End   193

John Douglas (J. D.) Williams shows off one of the specimens in the snake show at Paradise Park. Williams worked for more than thirty-three years with Ross Allen, catching, selling, and handling reptiles. Photo by Bruce Mozert. By permission of Bruce Mozert.

across a snake—even if it was a rattler—I would just give him room, go around him. I would always defend them and their right to live. I would tell people, 'Don't get lost too much in those stories, in those metaphors about the snake, the talking snake. Come on! Let's think about that.' Science was a part of that. For a long time I wanted to be a herpetologist. Even up to high school, I wanted to go to the University of Michigan and major in herpetology. In fact there was a man in Florida who had a place in Miami called Miami Serpentarium, a guy named Bill Haast. He worked with cobras. I wrote him when I was a junior in high school and told him about Uncle Son and told him when I got older I would love to work with him. Of course I got past that stage, but the science stayed with me, and when I went to college, I was originally going to teach, and one of my health teachers told me, 'You like science and math. You should go into public health,' and here I am. I became the first African American director of an immunization program in West Virginia. Every time I think of Uncle Son I am grateful. There was something key about what he did, how he stood out, how he followed his own journey. I always had a lot of respect for him. Just thinking about him brings tears to my eyes. The things that he stood for should be a part of Florida history. One person can make a difference. My Uncle Son affected the lives of many people. I can still

In 1973 Virginia Ferguson became the first woman boat driver hired at Silver Springs. As of 2015, she is still the captain of her own boat. Photo by Lu Vickers. By permission of Lu Vickers.

see him in the pit with those snakes. Telling stories about the snakes. Those snakes and alligators were part of my life."[42]

In 2015 Virginia Ferguson, aged seventy-three, was still going strong in her forty-first year as a boat captain on the Silver River. The single mother of four became the first woman captain at Silver Springs in 1973, and "some of the co-workers did not readily accept a woman of color in this job," she told a reporter in 2010. When the University of Central Florida did a short documentary on Ferguson, she talked about reactions people had to her. "When I first started, I would enter the back of the boat, and they would say 'Female captain, women's lib.' And I said, 'No, not women's lib. I have four children and we want to live. It has nothing to do with women's liberation.'"[43] She had survived worse during segregation; she could deal with a few misguided people.

When she cruised down the Fort King waterway past the old Paradise Park site, she discovered something terribly sad about the place she had loved.

"I went to Silver Springs in 1973 and Paradise Park was almost forgotten. You might cry when you go back there. It's almost like being raised up in a house and going away and coming back, and it's rundown and only the pillars are there. . . . We just forget so easily. Some people just want to forget it happened. But history is history; history is history and you can't take anything away from history. That's the way it was.

"We don't want to see it just go down the way it is. I went there with the wildlife staff. We found a piece of the slab, just a small piece of the slab and an old piece of a swing. There are a lot of people who don't know that Paradise Park ever existed. And then you always have your older seniors who come in and ask about Paradise Park, and sometimes that's all they want to talk about.

"I think they should make Paradise Park a part of Silver Springs, with the true history. Don't pull any punches. A lot of the history you read and hear is lies; people want to put a little paint on the woodwork. Tell it like it was; everybody has to live with it. Tell it like it was."[44]

Acknowledgments

We would like to thank the following people who helped with this book. First and foremost, a special thank you to the family of Mr. Eddie Leroy Vereen: Henrietta "Chippie" Vereen, Vivian Vereen Tillman, Sylvia Jones, Henry Jones, Reginald Lewis, Arizona Vereen-Turner, and Brenda Vereen. Thanks for sharing your stories and photographs. A huge thank you to Bruce Mozert, legendary photographer and Florida Treasure, who made many of the photographs documenting the history of Paradise Park. Thanks to the amazing Silver Springs boat captains: the late Willie Marsh, William Crowell, J. W. Culpepper, Nathaniel Thomas, Edgar Samuel, and Eddie Vereen, and to Roosevelt Faison, David Faison, Oscar Collins, Virginia Ferguson, Nathaniel "Pepper" Lewis, Riley Williams, and Leon Cheatom. You are the history of Silver Springs and one of the reasons Paradise Park came to be. Posthumous thanks to Carl Ray and Shorty Davidson for opening Paradise Park and to Thelma Parker and Pinkney Woodbury, activists and history keepers. Thanks to historian and journalist David Cook and to Scott Mitchell, Ricky Strow, and Guy Marwick of the Silver River Museum. Thanks to the late Joel Buchanan of the University of Florida's Smathers Library, the College of Central Florida, and the Florida Channel. A special thanks to each and every person who helped tell the story of Paradise Park with an interview, a photograph, a word of encouragement. Thanks to Mozert Studio, Adam Watson of the Florida Archives, the Smithsonian Institution, Temple University, Marion

County Black History Archives, the National Pastime Museum, the New York Public Library, and the Library of Congress for providing beautiful images. Thanks also to the people who read and critiqued the book: Gary Monroe, Tim Hollis, and Ben Swenson. Lu also thanks Meri Culp and Rebekka White for reading the book, providing additional feedback, and listening nonstop to all things Paradise. Thanks to the entire staff of the University Press of Florida for patience. Last but not least, we would each like to thank our families. Lu would like to thank her sons, Jordan, Samuel, and Elias, for supporting her writing. Cynthia would like to thank her husband, Ferdinand Graham, her children, Shameeka, Travis, and Howard, and her best friend, Monica Bryant.

Notes

Chapter 1. Paradise Park at Silver Springs

Epigraph source: Hurston, *Seraph on the Suwannee*, 334.

1. Johnnye Jacobs interview.

2. Monroe, "The Fate of Silver Springs."

3. Marian Rizzo, "A Silver Springs Story: Ricou Browning Was the Creature," *Ocala Star Banner*, July 18, 2013.

4. Berson, *Silver Springs*, 214–15.

5. David Cook, "Museum Complimented Indian Village," *Ocala Star Banner*, October 18, 1987.

6. Berson, *Silver Springs*, 214.

7. Roosevelt Faison interview.

8. Reginald Lewis interview.

9. Sheryl Murphy, "Eddie Vereen: Hall of Famer," *Challenger* 28, March 30, 1996.

10. Monte Martin, "Paradise Lost," *Ocala Magazine*, February 2005.

11. Luresa Lake interview.

12. Roosevelt Faison interview.

13. Dana Canedy, "Between the Lines, A Measure of Hurt," *New York Times*, June 29, 2000.

14. "Martin Andersen Tells Civic Leaders Silver Springs Holds Answer," *Ocala Star Banner*, May 29, 1949.

15. "The Road to Civil Rights," Highway History, *U.S. Department of Transportation Federal Highway Administration*, accessed June 18, 2014, https://www.fhwa.dot.gov/highwayhistory/road/s20.cfm.

16. "Martin Andersen Tells Civic Leaders."

17. Henry Jones interview.

18. "Black History at Mammoth Cave," National Park Service, http://www.nps.gov/maca/historyculture/black-history.htm.

19. Algeo, "Underground Tourists/Tourists Underground," 11.

20. Stowe, "A Sail into Fairyland."

21. Bok, letter to the directors.

22. Stan Windhorn, "Ocala Takes Lead in Providing Recreational Facilities for Negroes," *Sarasota Herald Tribune*, September 4, 1956.

23. Marian Rizzo, "Paradise Park Was a Haven for Black Community," *Ocala Star Banner*, August 22, 2013.

24. Henry Jones interview.

25. Edgar Samuel interview.

26. Monte Martin, "Paradise Lost," *Ocala Magazine,* February 2005.

27. Susan Latham Carr, "Ocala's Own Paradise," *Ocala Star Banner,* February 28, 1993.

28. Timothy Green interview.

29. Windhorn, "Ocala Takes Lead."

30. Berson, *Silver Springs*, 256.

31. Jonothon King, "Mack King Carter: The Voice and the Vision," *Sun Sentinel*, August 27, 1989.

32. Mack King Carter interview.

33. McCloud Raines Jr. interview.

34. Nathaniel "Pepper" Lewis interview.

35. Michael McLeod, "'I Want You to Raise Them, Dolly,'" *Orlando Sentinel,* October 18, 1998.

36. Brenda Vereen interview.

37. Windhorn, "Ocala Takes Lead."

38. Brenda Vereen interview.

39. Carol Croskey interview.

40. Reginald Lewis interview.

41. Henry Jones interview.

42. Sylvia Jones interview.

43. Henry Jones interview.

44. Johnnye Jacobs interview.

45. Doris Jacobs-Smith interview.

46. Arizona Vereen-Turner interview.

47. Reginald Lewis interview.

48. Monica Bryant, "Paradise Lost," *Ocala Star Banner,* February 5, 2006.

49. Lashonda Stinson, "A Fitting Memorial," *Ocala Star Banner,* May 22, 2003.

50. Sylvia Jones interview.

51. Vivian Vereen Tillman interview.

52. Sheryl Murphy, "Eddie Vereen: Hall of Famer," *Challenger* 28, March 30, 1996.

53. Dr. Dorsey Miller interview.

54. David Rackard interview.

55. "Scout Leaders Map Expansion," *St. Petersburg Times,* December 23, 1950.

56. "Red" Turner, "Natural Wildlife Area Serves as Setting for Scouts," *Ocala Star Banner*, October 16, 1963.

57. Virginia Ferguson interview.

Chapter 2. Seminoles and African Americans in Marion County

Epigraph sources: Charles Dunning, "In a Florida Cracker's Cabin," *Lippincott Magazine* 29, New Series 3, January 1882; Hurston, *Color Struck*, 38.

1. "West Ocala History," *Historic Ocala*, March 21, 2013, http://www.ocalafl.org/historic/HO3.aspx?id=346.

2. Joseph Opala, "Black Seminoles—Gullahs Who Escaped from Slavery," *The Gullah: Rice, Slavery, and the Sierra Leone-American Connection*, http://yale.edu/glc/gullah/07.htm.

3. "Florida of the Seminoles," Florida History Internet Center, accessed October 21, 2014, http://floridahistory.org/seminoles.htm.

4. McCall, *Letters from the Frontiers*.

5. "West Ocala History," Historic Ocala, accessed March 15, 2013, http://www.ocalafl.org/historic/HO3.aspx?id=346.

6. Ott and Chazal, *Ocali Country*, 147.

7. Diane Daniel, "The Men to See for Florida Memorabilia," *Boston Globe*, February 3, 2013.

8. Chris Mayhew, "Henry Coppinger, Jr." *Codiaeum Connection*, July 2011, 14–15, http://www.palmpedia.net/wiki/HENRY_COPPINGER_JR.

9. David Cook, "Seminole Village Popular at Silver Springs," *Ocala Star Banner*, February 9, 2014.

10. Martin, *Eternal Spring*.

11. Daniel, "The Men to See."

12. Bill Bolus, "Lewis Plantation Recalls Heyday of Old South," *St. Petersburg Times*, February 19, 1956.

13. "Turpentine Plantation," *Milwaukee Journal*, January 2, 1949.

14. West, *The Enduring Seminoles*, 56.

15. "Ross Allen Reptile Institute," video, 13:30, http://www.floridamemory.com/items/show/232386.

16. "The Tourist Camps," Ah-Tah-Thi-Ki Seminole Indian Museum, podcast audio, http://www.ahtahthiki.com/Home-Seminole-Tribe-Florida-Ah-Tah-Thi-Ki-Museum.html.

17. Buculavas et al., *South Florida Folklife*.

18. Marion Brown, "Sculptress Finds Art Is Staging a Comeback," *Evening Independent*, January 14, 1939.

19. Scott, "Official Language, Unofficial Reality," 194–95.

20. "West Ocala History," *Historic Ocala*, accessed March 15, 2013, http://www.ocalafl.org/historic/HO3.aspx?id=346.

21. Dr. Dorsey Miller interview.

22. Thelma Parker, "Remembering a 'Liberator' during Black History Month," *Ocala Star Banner*, February 14, 1996.

23. "West Ocala History."

24. "Gadson's," advertisement, *Ocala Evening Star,* June 18, 1908. http://ufdci-mages.uflib.ufl.edu/UF/00/07/59/08/00874/0546.pdf.

25. Harriet Daniels, "Picturing the Past," *Ocala Star Banner,* February 26, 2002.

26. Wayne Nielsen interview.

27. "Colored Board Trade Meeting," *Miami Herald,* November 30, 1915.

28. *Crisis,* November 1917.

29. Wilson and Peck, *St. Petersburg's Historic 22nd Street South.*

30. Quoted in Jackson, *Booker T. Washington and the Struggle,* 163, 165.

31. Gail Pellett and Bill Moyers, *Songs Are Free: Bernice Johnson Reagon and African American Music,* documentary film aired on PBS, 1991.

32. Thelma Parker, "Howard Academy and Howard High School Had Interesting History," *Ocala Star Banner,* June 29, 1994; on land and early teachers see Louis Chazal, "The Kingdom of the Sun: Part II," *Ocala Star Banner,* December 30, 1958.

33. LaRone Taylor Davis interview.

34. Susan Latham Carr, "Memories of the Past," *Ocala Star Banner,* February 27, 2000.

35. Monica Bryant, "Simpler Times," *Ocala Star Banner*, February 12, 2006.

36. Walker, *Their Highest Potential.*

37. Loretta Pompey Jenkins interview.

38. Harriet Daniels, "Picturing the Past," *Ocala Star Banner*, February 26, 2002.

39. Laura Kauffmann, "Mission Well Done," *Ocala Star Banner,* February 28, 1996.

40. Carlos Medina, "A Place in History," *Ocala Star Banner,* February 26, 1996.

41. Green, *Before His Time.*

42. Dr. Clarence Cotton interview.

43. "War Memorial Swim Program Attracts 100," *Ocala Star Banner,* June 23, 1955.

44. Dr. Clarence Cotton interview.

45. "Killins, Mrs. Susie Long. Obituary," *Ocala Star Banner*, July 30, 1985.

46. Guy McCarthy, "Pinkney Woodbury Faces Change Head on," *Ocala Star Banner*, February 20, 1994.

47. Susan Latham Carr, "Tucker Hill Revitalization Is Underway," *Ocala Star Banner*, April 25, 2012.

48. Michael McLeod, "'I Want You to Raise Them, Dolly,'" *Orlando Sentinel,* October 18, 1998.

49. Thomas Francis, "Witch Hunt at New Mount Olive," *Broward Palm Beach New Times*, December 20, 2007.

50. Austin Long interview.

51. Bridget Hall, "Legacy of Service," *Ocala Star Banner*, February 14, 1999.

52. "Whispering Pines," *Ocala Evening Star,* December 10, 1908, http://fl-genweb.org/mpc/marion/whispering%20pines/transwhispering.html.

53. Dr. Clarence Cotton interview.

54. Henry Jones interview.

55. Julius Stafford, "Town Talk," *Ocala Star Banner,* January 8, 1963.

56. Arizona Vereen-Turner interview.

57. Andy Fillmore, "After 50 Years, Woman Still Fighting for Civil Rights," *Ocala Star Banner*, February 1, 2014.

58. Johnnye Jacobs interview; Doris Jacobs-Smith interview.

59. Doris Jacobs-Smith interview.

60. Virginia Ferguson interview.

61. Luresa Lake interview.

62. Stone, *Sacred Steel*.

63. Harriet Daniels, "A Rare Pearl," *Ocala Star Banner*, May 31, 1997.

64. Brenda Flynn interview.

Chapter 3. African American History at Silver Springs: A River Runs through It

Epigraph source: Boyd Fisher, "From the Atlantic to the Gulf through Florida's Inland Waterways," *Motorboating*, January 1927.

1. Willie Marsh interview.

2. Bass, *When Steamboats Reigned in Florida*.

3. Norton, *Handbook of Florida*, 297.

4. Charles Dunning, "In a Florida Cracker's Cabin," *Lippincott Magazine* 29, New Series 3, January 1882.

5. "'It's a Long John': Traditional African-American Work Songs," *History Matters*, http://historymatters.gmu.edu/d/5758/.

6. Dunning, "In a Florida Cracker's Cabin."

7. Lanier, *Florida*, 30.

8. John Somerville and Ella Teague DeBerard, "Steamboats in the Hyacinths," *Ocala Star Banner*, May 1, 1955.

9. Leon Cheatom interview.

10. Willie Marsh and William Crowell interview.

11. Dan Guido, "World Looks More Clear in Sparkling Silver," *Ocala Star Banner*, July 26, 1983.

12. Martin, *Eternal Spring*.

13. Ramsey, *The Luffmans*.

14. Ott and Chazal, *Ocali Country*.

15. Martin, *Eternal Spring*.

16. Willie Marsh and William Crowell interview.

17. Ramsey, *The Luffmans*.

18. Guido, "World Looks More Clear."

19. David Cook, "Visionary Developed Silver Springs," *Ocala Star Banner*, March 30, 1997.

20. Guido, "World Looks More Clear."

21. Willie Marsh and William Crowell interview.

22. "Veteran Guide at Silver Springs to Retire," *Ocala Star Banner*, March 27, 1966.

23. Guido, "World Looks More Clear."

24. Henry Jones interview.

25. "Silver Springs Daylight Route," brochure.

26. Ibid.

27. Jennifer Miller, "Something Ghostly This Way Comes," *Ocala Star Banner*, October 27, 2003.

28. Dr. Joyce Hope Scott interview.

29. Willie Marsh and William Crowell interview.

30. Sylvia Jones interview.

31. Willie Marsh and William Crowell interview.

32. Dianne Perrine, "Special Recognition," *Ocala Star Banner*, February 20, 2001.

Chapter 4. *The Ray and Davidson Era*

Epigraph source: Hardy Croom, quoted in David Cook, "Man Has Seen Changes in Silver Springs," *Ocala Star Banner*, July 4, 1993.

1. Martin, *Eternal Spring*.

2. Hollis, *Glass Bottom Boats and Mermaid Tails*.

3. Dan Guido, "World Looks More Clear in Sparkling Silver," *Ocala Star Banner*, July 26 1983.

4. Martin, *Eternal Spring*.

5. David Cook, "M. R. Porter Details New Plans for New Paradise Park," *Ocala Star Banner*, February 11, 1996.

6. David Cook, "Paradise Park Problem Finally Resolved," *Ocala Star Banner*, March 3, 1996.

7. "Paradise Park," brochure.

8. Cook, "Paradise Park Problem Finally Resolved."

9. Hollis, *Glass Bottom Boats and Mermaid Tails*.

10. "Coolidge Kept His Mouth Shut," *Ocala Star Banner*, August 7, 1970.

11. "He Logs Thousands of Miles as Boat Captain Close to Port," *Ocala Star Banner*, July 2, 1963.

12. Willie Marsh and William Crowell interview.

13. David Cook, "Museum Complimented Indian Village," *Ocala Star Banner*, October 18, 1987.

14. Guido, "World Looks More Clear."

15. Nathaniel "Pepper" Lewis interview.

16. Henry Jones interview.

17. Willie Marsh and William Crowell interview.

18. Jessica Green, "Ocala Avenue Christened for Couple Who Touched Many," *Ocala Star Banner*, May 10, 2008.

Chapter 5. *African Americans in Florida's Tourist Industry*

Epigraph source: Lorna Carroll, "The Bard of Rainbow Springs," *St. Petersburg Times*, March 28, 1960.

1. "Roadside Attractions in Florida: Tourism and Spectacle before Disney," Florida Memory project, http://www.floridamemory.com/photographiccollection/photo_exhibits/roadside-attractions/.

2. Frank Ceresi and Carol McMains, "Original Photo of the 1885–1886 Cuban Giants: Baseball's First Professional Team," *The National Pastime Museum*, http://www.thenationalpastimemuseum.com/article/original-photo-1885-1886 -cuban-giants-black-baseballs-first-professional-team.

3. Stuart McIver, "Cooks to Catchers, Bellhops to Batters," *Ft. Lauderdale Sun Sentinel*, August 22, 1993.

4. Urlin, *Dancing Ancient and Modern*.

5. Stearns and Stearns, *Jazz Dance*, 22.

6. "Palm Beach Cake Walks," *New York Times*, February 15, 1903.

7. "Negro Tourists Arriving Too," *Evening Independent*, March 7, 1929.

8. "At Ponte Vedra Beach," *New York Times*, November 8, 1942.

9. Eliot Kleinberg, "Afromobile an Offensive Coinage tor the 'Chariots' of Palm Beach," Historic Palm Beach blog, *Palm Beach Post*. http://historicpalm beach.blog.palmbeachpost.com/2000/04/12/afromobile-an-offensive-coinage -for-the-chariots-of-palm-b/.

10. Gary Enos, "West Palm Pioneer Dies at 99: Dr. Alice F. Mickens a 'God-mother' to Many," *Ft. Lauderdale Sun Sentinel*. January 20, 1988.

11. "'Negro Day' Excursion Set," *St. Petersburg Times*, April 19, 1952.

12. Henry Louis Gates Jr., "What Was America's 1st Black Town?" December 31, 2012, *The Root*, http://www.theroot.com/articles/history/2012/12/what_ was_americas_first_black_town_100_amazing_facts_about_the_negro.html.

13. Marcia Lane, "Butler Beach's beginnings," *St. Augustine Register*, February 1, 2007.

14. David Nolan, "A Moment in Black History: Major Argrett," *St. Augustine Record*, February 5, 2003.

15. "Surreys Survive in Oldest City," *Ebony*, August 1946, 11–14.

16. David Nolan, "A Moment in Black History: Major Argrett," *St. Augustine Record*, February 5, 2003.

17. Hezekiah Butterworth, "Excursion Life in Florida," *Chautauquan* 10, 1890.

18. Jeff Klinkenberg, "Wakulla Springs Isn't as Clear as It Used to Be, but Musical Tour Guides Carry on," *Tampa Bay Times*, March 27, 2009.

19. Kevin Canty, "Big Fun in North Florida: Florida," *New York Times*, November 10, 1996.

20. Klinkenberg, "Wakulla Springs."

21. Hemenway, *Zora Neale Hurston*, 91.

22. "Vaulting Fish," *St. Petersburg Times*, February 5, 1958.

23. Lorna Carroll, "The Bard of Rainbow Springs," *St. Petersburg Times*, March 28, 1960.

24. Holly Mulkey, "Lincolnville: Remembering a Lincolnville Legend," March 28, 2013, *St. Augustine Record*, http://staugustine.com/living/neighbors/2013-03-27/ lincolnville-remembering-lincolnville-legend#.VGYwE2etx8E.

25. "ACCORD Freedom Trail—120 DeHaven Street," *Waymark*, accessed January 3, 2015, http://www.waymarking.com/waymarks/WMGC2J.

26. Perkins, *Aunt Aggie's Bone Yard*.

27. "Only Negro Lion Tamer," *Ebony*, October 1964, 49–55.

28. "Obituary and Update for 'Junior' Ruffin," Circus Fans Association of

America, accessed September 24, 2010, http://www.circusfans.org/news_detail.php?news_id=2591.

29. "History of Overtown's Lyric Theater," Black Archives History and Research Foundation of South Florida, accessed September 25, 2013, http://www.theblackarchives.org/?page_id=734.

30. John Dudley, "Where Is Dana Albert Dorsey?" *South Florida Times,* June 11, 2010, http://www.sfltimes.com/uncategorized/where-is-dana-albert-dorsey.

31. "Black Pioneer's Dorsey Hotel Gone in a Blaze," *Miami News,* January 22, 1981.

32. "They Developed the Springs," *Ocala Star Banner,* May 30, 1962.

33. Quoted in Susan Latham Carr, "Ocala's Own Paradise," *Ocala Star Banner,* February 28, 1993.

Chapter 6. "South of the South"

Epigraph source: Howard, *Lynchings,* 23.

1. "Florida, the Land of Sunshine."
2. "Warning to Florida Tourists," *American Mercury,* June 1925.
3. King, *Devil in the Grove,* 105, 108.
4. Eric Ericson, "Dead Wrong," *Orlando Weekly,* October 1, 1998.
5. King, *Devil in the Grove,* 358, 359.
6. Edmond Fordham interview.
7. Dr. Robert W. Saunders Sr. interview.
8. Edmond Fordham interview.
9. Bud Crussell, "Marshall Tackled Tough Case in Ocala, Attorney Recalls," *Ocala Star Banner,* January 26, 2003.
10. King, *Devil in the Grove.*
11. Eloisa Ruano Gonzales, "Groveland Four Relatives Receive Response from State, but No Apology," *Orlando Sentinel,* August 13, 2012.
12. "Miami Success Climaxes Storybook Career," *Ebony,* May 1, 1951, 76.
13. "A Beachhead in Miami," *Ebony,* March 1951, 96–97.
14. Biondi, *Miami Beach Memories,* 30.
15. Bernard Kahn, "Louis-Graves Bout Here Delayed Until Tonight," *Daytona Beach Morning Journal,* February 3, 1949.
16. Jody Benjamin, "Past Glory Fades into History: The Hampton House Motel, Once a Bustling Hangout That Attracted Celebrities to the Black Community in Miami, Today Lies in Ruins," *Sun-Sentinel,* February 18, 2001.
17. Andres Viglucci, "Historic Hampton House Motel, Part of Miami's Black History, Breaks Ground on Restoration Project," *Miami Herald,* May 23, 2013.
18. Historic Hampton House Community Trust, accessed January 3, 2015, http://www.historichamptonhousemiami.org/index.html.
19. "Official Group Given Pre-View of Paradise Park." *Ocala Star Banner,* May 19, 1949.
20. Advertisement for Paradise Park, *Ocala Star Banner,* May 16, 1968.
21. "Paradise Park on Silver River to Open Friday," *Ocala Star Banner,* May 19, 1949.

22. David Cook, "City Leaders Disappointed by Low Census Count in 1950," *Ocala Star Banner*, April 29, 2000.

23. Davies, *Sports in American Life*.

Chapter 7. Segregated Summers

Epigraph source: "Atlantic Coast Has Most Negro Summer Resorts," *Ebony*, July, 1947, 16–17.

1. "Landmark Legislation: Civil Rights Act of 1875," United States Senate, accessed August 3, 2013, https://www.senate.gov/artandhistory/history/common/generic/CivilRightsAct1875.htm.

2. DuBois, *Black Reconstruction in America*, 110.

3. Levine, *Black Culture and Black Consciousness*, 263.

4. "Landmark Legislation."

5. "Plessy v. Ferguson (1896)," *Our Documents*, accessed August 3, 2013, http://www.ourdocuments.gov/doc.php?flash=true&doc=52.

6. Woodward, *The Strange Career of Jim Crow*, 17.

7. "Answering Mr. Bradley: Colored People at Asbury Park Speak Out in Meeting," *New York Times*, June 28, 1887.

8. "The Color Line at Asbury Park: Visitors Annoyed by Colored Servants on the Beach," *New York Times*, June 30, 1889.

9. Goldberg, "Greetings from Jim Crow, New Jersey."

10. "The Chicago Race Riot of 1919," *History.com*, accessed August 3, 2013, http://www.history.com/topics/black-history/chicago-race-riot-of-1919.

11. Quoted in Ronald J. Stephens, "Chicken Bone Beach, Atlantic City, New Jersey (1900–)," Blackpast.org, accessed August 3, 2013, http://www.blackpast.org/aah/chicken-bone-beach-atlantic-city-new-jersey-1900#sthash.XGP0Fr4Y.lufENVK7.dpuf.

12. Quoted in Jeannette Wood, "African Americans Remember Glamour and Separation in A. C.'s past," *Newsworks*, accessed August 30, 2013, http://www.newsworks.org/index.php/local/new-jersey/59179-african-americans-remember-glamour-and-separation-in-acs-past.

13. Bill Kent, "Refusing to Forget the Pain of Racism," *New York Times*, August 31, 1997.

14. Eryn Jelesiewicz, "Photos Give Inside View of African-American Life from 1930s to 1960s," Temple University News Center, accessed June 13, 2012, http://news.temple.edu/news/2012-06-13/photos-give-inside-view-african-american-life-1930s-1960s.

15. "'Green Book' Helped African-Americans Travel Safely," Neal Conan, *Talk of the Nation*, NPR, September 15, 2010, http://www.npr.org/templates/story/story.php?storyId=129885990.

16. Green, *The Negro Traveler's Green Book*.

17. Rugh, *Are We There Yet?*, 78.

18. Brigham Young University, "Black Family Vacations in the 1950s: An Untold Story," news release, February 12, 2008, http://news.byu.edu/archive08-Feb-blackvacations.aspx.

19. Stan Windhorn, "Ocala Takes Lead in Providing Recreational Facilities for Negroes," *Sarasota Herald Tribune.* September 4, 1956.

20. Sylvia Jones interview.

21. Amelia Pinkston interview.

22. Mary Carolyn Williams interview.

23. Jenny Hammer, "Bali Motor Inn and Club Bali," *Ocala Star Banner*, July 26, 2010.

24. Celia McGee, "The Open Road Wasn't Quite Open to All," *New York Times,* August 22, 2010.

25. "Juanita Cunningham," *Ocala Star Banner*, February 25, 2013.

26. Monica Bryant, "'Courageous' Friends, Family Recall Area Civil Rights Pioneer," *Ocala Star Banner*, February 26, 2006.

27. Doak, *The March on Washington*, 41.

28. Kenneth Jones interview.

29. Audrey Peterson, "Sag Harbor Works to Save History," *Hamptons Magazine*, accessed July 25, 2013, http://hamptons-magazine.com/lifestyle/articles/sag-harbor-african-american-communities.

30. Whitehead, *Sag Harbor,* 24.

31. "'Black Eden': The Town That Segregation Built," Amy Robinson, *Morning Edition*, NPR, July 5, 2012, http://www.npr.org/2012/07/05/156089624/black-eden-the-town-that-segregation-built.

32. Erica Taylor, "Little Known Black History Fact: Nick Gabaldon, The Black Surfer," *BlackAmericaWeb*, September 9, 2013, http://blackamericaweb.com/2013/09/09/little-known-black-history-fact-nick-gabaldon-the-black-surfer/.

33. "Shearer Cottage's History on Martha's Vineyard," *Shearer Cottage,* accessed September 12, 2013, http://www.shearercottage.com/history.php.

34. Karhl, *The Land Was Ours.*

35. Eugene Meyer, "A Welcoming Enclave with Roots in a Snub," *New York Times,* September 4, 2009.

36. Chris Schaad, "Bizarre History of Cape May: Cape May History Not Immune to Slavery," *Cape May Gazette,* April 5, 2013.

37. *Crisis,* April 1911.

38. "Bruce's Beach, Manhattan Beach, California (1920–)," Blackpast.org, accessed September 12, 2013, http://www.blackpast.org/aaw/bruce-s-beach-manhattan-beach-california-1920#sthash.LRFt2R2u.dpuf.

39. "Bruce's Beach Celebration 2007," YouTube video, 1:07, posted by the City Project, July 25, 2007, https://www.youtube.com/watch?v=yMDWxDtwE1s.

40. Norris McDonald, "Save Freeman Beach," African American Environmentalist Association, July 8, 2010, http://aaenvironment.blogspot.com/2010/07/save-freeman-beach.html.

41. Herbert L. White, "Oceanside Divide," *Our State: North Carolina,* accessed June 18, 2014, https://www.ourstate.com/oceanside-divide/.

42. Emma Vereen, Earlene Woods, and Ronald Isom, "The Black Pearl," Town of Atlantic Beach, S.C., accessed August 3, 2013, http://townofatlanticbeachsc.com/uploads/Atlantic_Beach_History_Brochure_1.pdf.

43. Jeffrey Collins, "The Nation," *Los Angeles Times,* February 1, 2009.

44. Vereen et al., "The Black Pearl."

Chapter 8. Divided Beaches

Epigraph sources: "The Magic of the Gulf Stream," advertisement for Flagler's East Coast Railroad, *Montreal Gazette,* December 4, 1926; Pablo Beach 1924 ordinance quoted in Mabry, *World's Finest Beach,* 82.

1. "Board Threatens to Sell Beaches," *St. Petersburg Times,* October 25, 1955.

2. Maxwell, "Angry Young Man," 8–17, quotes at 12, 14.

3. Bill Maxwell interview.

4. Josh, "Have You Heard of Milwaukee Springs?" *The Florida Memory Blog,* Florida Memory project, June 16, 2014, http://www.floridamemory.com/blog/2014/06/16/have-you-heard-of-milwaukee-springs/.

5. Stan Windhorn, "Delray Beach to Provide Negro Recreational Facilities," *Sarasota Herald Tribune,* September 5, 1956.

6. Stan Windhorn, "Negroes' Jupiter Beach in Palm Beach Aid to Harmony," *Sarasota Herald-Tribune,* September 6, 1956.

7. Stan Windhorn, "Racial Harmony Exists in Jacksonville's Recreation," *Sarasota Herald Tribune,* September 2, 1956.

8. "Negroes Oppose Pool, Ask for Public Beach," *Sarasota Herald Tribune,* June 18, 1955.

9. William Crawford Jr., "The Long Hard Fight for Equal Rights: A History of Broward County's Colored Beach and Fort Lauderdale's Beach 'Wade-ins" of the Summer of 1961," accessed August 3, 2013, http://www.floridasbigdig.com/uploads/ColoredBeachWadeInTequesta0001.pdf.

10. Don Mizell, "Mizell More Fitting Name for Historic Beach," *Sun Sentinel,* December 14, 2011.

11. Cynthia Roby, "Wade in the Water," *South Florida Times,* April 10, 2008.

12. Scott Wyman, "Fort Lauderdale Breaks Ground on Museum for Civil Rights Leader Eula Johnson," *Ft. Lauderdale Sun-Sentinel,* March 8, 2011.

13. Tom Swick, "The Mizells, A Medical History," *Ft. Lauderdale Magazine,* May 8, 2013.

14. Mizell, "Mizell More Fitting Name."

15. Susan Laird, "American Beach Fights to Preserve a Place in History," *Ocala Star Banner,* January 21, 1995.

16. McCarthy, *African American Sites in Florida,* 183.

17. Laird, "American Beach Fights."

18. Rymer, *American Beach.*

19. Quoted in Carolyn Williams, "History of American Beach: 1964, Beginning of the End," http://www.nps.gov/timu/historyculture/ambch_beginningofend.htm.

20. Williams, "History of American Beach."

21. "Florida's First Negro Resort," *Ebony,* February 1948, 24–26.

22. Albert Bethune interview.

23. "Florida's First Negro Resort," *Ebony,* February 1948, 24–26.

24. "Historically Black Beach Disappears with Integration," *Florida Times-Union,* October 12, 2003.

25. Eleanor Roosevelt, "My Day: March 20, 1953," http://www.gwu.edu/~erpapers/myday/displaydoc.cfm?_y=1953&_f=md002487.

26. Mary McLeod Bethune, "Thousands Flock to Bethune-Volusia Beach: Answer to a 34-Year Dream," *New York Age,* August 2, 1952.

27. Lamb, *Blackout,* 89–92.

28. Albert Bethune interview.

29. Smith, *Mary McLeod Bethune.*

30. John McCann, "Blacks Enjoy a Better Day on Beach," *Orlando Sentinel,* April 10, 2002.

31. Matt Grimson, "Historically Black Beach Disappears with Integration," *Daytona Beach News-Journal,* October 13, 2003.

32. "Welcome to Bethune Beach," http://www.bethunebeachfl.com/.

33. Ginelle Torres, "Beachhead for Black History," *Sun Sentinel,* December 26, 2004.

34. Adrian Sainz, "Historic Virginia Key Beach Seeks National Status," *Florida Times-Union,* September 28, 2002.

Chapter 9. Paradise Found

Epigraph source: "Paradise Park," brochure, Collection of Lu Vickers.

1. Bill "Blue" Ray interview.

2. James Curley Sr. interview.

3. Nathaniel "Pepper" Lewis interview.

4. Marian Rizzo, "Paradise Park Was a Haven for Black Community," *Ocala Star Banner,* August 22, 2013.

5. Leon Cheatom interview.

6. Roosevelt Faison interview.

7. Susan Latham Carr, "Ocala's Own Paradise," *Ocala Star Banner*, February 28, 1993.

8. Arizona Vereen-Turner interview.

9. Rizzo, "Paradise Park Was a Haven."

10. Reginald Lewis interview.

11. Rizzo, "Paradise Park Was a Haven."

12. Sylvia Jones interview.

13. "'Negro Day' Excursion Set," *St. Petersburg Times,* April 19, 1952.

14. "Ticket Sales Increase for Paradise Park Tour," *St. Petersburg Times*, May 24, 1952.

15. Reginald Lewis interview.

16. Sylvia Jones interview.

17. Reginald Lewis interview.

18. Johnnye Jacobs and Doris Jacobs-Smith interviews.

19. Samuel Crosby interview.

20. Bill Bryant, "How About Some Alligator Soup, or Snake Meat," *Ocala Star Banner*, July 6, 1958.

21. Samuel Crosby interview.

22. Naomi Crosby interview.

23. Robert Hunter, "Willie's Philosophy in Snake Pit," *Daytona Beach Morning Journal*, March 24, 1953.

24. "Doc Sausage: The Recordings of Lucious "Dr. Sausage" Tyson," *The Archivist Presents*, accessed August 21, 2013, http://thearchivistpresents.blogspot.com/2012/09/doc-sausage-recordings-of-lucious-dr.html.

25. Henry Jones interview.

26. Wiltse, *Contested Waters*, 78.

27. "Racial History of American Swimming Pools," interview by Rachel Martin with Jeff Wiltse, *The Bryant Park Project*, NPR, May 6, 2008, http://www.npr.org/templates/story/story.php?storyId=90213675.

28. Stan Windhorn, "Ocala Takes Lead in Providing Recreational Facilities for Negroes," *Sarasota Herald Tribune*, September 4, 1956.

29. Henry Jones interview.

30. Tommy Brooks interview.

31. Andy Fillmore, "Ramah Missionary Baptist Celebrates 120th Anniversary," *Ocala Star Banner*, October 29, 2012.

32. Mayo Faison interview.

33. Gloria Johnson Pasteur interview.

34. David Faison interview.

35. Nathaniel "Pepper" Lewis interview.

36. Henry Jones interview.

37. Whitfield Jenkins interview.

38. "Paradise Park," brochure.

39. Bruce Mozert interview.

40. Luresa Lake interview.

41. Leroy Roundtree interview.

42. "Legion Sponsors Beauties Contest in Paradise Park," *Evening Independent*, September 2, 1949.

43. Gloria Johnson Pasteur interview.

44. Carrie Parker-Warren interview.

45. LaRone Taylor Davis interview.

46. Green, *Before His Time*.

47. Virginia Ferguson interview.

48. Julius Stafford, "Town Talk," *Ocala Star Banner*, September 11, 1962.

49. "Jackie Robinson Planning Ocala Address Saturday," *St. Petersburg Times*, February 7, 1964.

50. Henry Jones interview.

51. Edgar Samuel interview.

52. Mary McLeod Bethune, "Easter Monday of 1950 Was My Day of Reaping," *Chicago Defender*, April 29, 1950.

53. Albert Bethune interview.

54. Sylvia Jones interview.

55. "Town Talk," *Ocala Star Banner,* April 18, 1963.

56. Joe Callahan, "Making History," *Ocala Star Banner*, June 18, 2000.

57. Bill Maxwell interview.

58. Virginia Ferguson interview.

59. "Underwater Fairyland Park's Biggest Attraction," *Ebony,* March 1953.

60. Bill Thompson, "Ocala—It was a tourist-luring device, common and familiar today," *Ocala Star Banner,* June 7, 2001.

61. Freddie Lee Perkins interview.

62. Brenda Vereen interview.

63. Narvella Haynes interview.

64. Carol Croskey interview.

65. Henry Jones interview.

66. Arizona Vereen-Turner interview.

67. Samuel Crosby interview.

68. Oscar Collins interview.

69. Dr. Dorsey Miller interview.

70. Roosevelt Faison interview.

71. Quoted in Susan Latham Carr, "Ocala's Own Paradise," *Ocala Star Banner*, February 28, 1993.

72. Jim Moorhead, "Sale of Silver Springs Confirmed," *Ocala Star Banner,* May 29, 1962.

73. "Merited Recognition," *Ocala Star Banner,* December 10, 1959.

74. Frank Slayton, "Silver Springs Phoenix Rises from Own Embers," *Lakeland Ledger*, July 21, 1957.

75. "Underwater Theater Adds New Vistas at Florida Springs," *Milwaukee Sentinel*, January 6, 1962.

76. Willie Marsh and William Crowell interview.

Chapter 10. The Beginning of the End

Epigraph source: Don Pride, "NAACP Units Picket Together," *St. Petersburg Times,* August 2, 1963.

1. Don Meiklejohn, "Negro Harassment Is Alleged," *St. Petersburg Times,* September 24, 1963.

2. "Rep. Bryant Takes Stand for Segregation in Tampa Speech," *Ocala Star Banner,* January 26, 1956.

3. "Police Seek Men in Ocala Shooting," *St. Petersburg Times,* July 29, 1963.

4. Mary Carolyn Williams interview.

5. Lystra Mulzac, "Hunting and Fishing Club Had a Purpose," *Ocala Star Banner,* October 23, 1989.

6. Monica Bryant, "'Courageous' Friends, Family Recall Area Civil Rights Pioneer," *Ocala Star Banner,* February 26, 2006.

7. L. C. Stevenson interview.

8. Bryant, "'Courageous' Friends."

9. Dr. Dorsey Miller interview.

10. "The Beginning of the End of Segregation in Richmond," *History Replays Today,* February 19, 2012, http://www.historyreplaystoday.com/2012/02/the-begining-of-end-of-segregation-in.html.

11. David Rackard interview.

12. Dr. Dorsey Miller interview; L. C. Stevenson interview.

13. Dr. Clarence Cotton interview.

14. Quoted in Bryant, "'Courageous' Friends."

15. Dr. Dorsey Miller interview.

16. Donald Pride, "U.S. Said Eying Arrests in Florida," *St. Petersburg Times*, July 27, 1963.

17. Andy Fillmore, "After 50 years, Woman Still Fighting for Civil Rights," *Ocala Star Banner,* February 1, 2014.

18. R. Hart Phillips, "Racial Protests Stir Ocala, FLA," *New York Times,* July 26, 1963.

19. J. A Dunn, "Generations of Progress," *Ocala Star Banner,* February 1, 1998.

20. Pride, "U.S. Said Eying Arrests."

21. "Leader Pledges to Fill Jails," *Lakeland Ledger,* August 1, 1963.

22. "Florida NAACP Militants Chain-Whipped by KKK," Stetson Kennedy Collection, *Civil Rights Library of St. Augustine,* accessed August 21, 2013, http://civilrightslibrary.com/.

23. Patrick Donges, "50 Years of the Civil Rights Act: Dr. Robert B. Hayling," *WJCT News,* July 1, 2014.

24. "Timeline," Civil Rights Library of St. Augustine, accessed August 21, 2013, http://civilrightslibrary.com/timeline/.

25. "Acid Reception," *Spokane Daily Chronicle,* June 19, 1964.

26. Laura Kauffmann, "District Doubles Minority Hires, Still Has Long Way to Go," *Ocala Star Banner,* August 2, 1996.

27. Whitfield Jenkins interview.

28. "Paradise Pk. Opens," *Ocala Star Banner,* May 20, 1968.

29. Reginald Lewis interview.

30. "Town Talk," *Ocala Star Banner,* April 18, 1963.

31. Riley Williams interview.

32. Roosevelt Faison interview.

33. David Cook, "Strong Effort Fails to Reroute I-75 through Downtown Ocala—Ocalans Reluctantly Accept I-75 Route," *Ocala Star Banner,* January 2, 2005.

34. Nathaniel "Pepper" Lewis interview.

35. Dr. Clarence Cotton interview.

36. "Depression Saviour . . . Springs Proved Pot of Gold," *Ocala Star Banner,* February 1, 1976.

37. Dr. Dorsey Miller interview.

38. Brenda Vereen interview.

39. Roosevelt Faison interview.

40. Ed Garland, "Capturing an Oral History of Florida's Springs: Experiences Enhance Understanding of Science," Southeast Volusia Audubon Society,

February 2014, http://www.sevolusiaaudubon.org/eskimmer/feb2014_sjrwmd. html.

41. Monica Bryant, "Paradise Lost," *Ocala Star Banner*, February 5, 2006.

42. Samuel Crosby interview.

43. "One Short: Silver Springs," University of Central Florida, May 29, 2013, https://www.youtube.com/watch?v=RtuvVjDbfuk.

44. Virginia Ferguson interview.

Notes to Pages 193–196

Bibliography

Algeo, Katie. "Underground Tourists/Tourists Underground: African American Tourism to Mammoth Cave." *Tourism Geographies: An International Journal of Tourism Space, Place and Environment,* April 13, 2012.

Bass, Bob. *When Steamboats Reigned in Florida.* Gainesville: University Press of Florida, 2008.

Berson, Thomas. *Silver Springs: The Florida Interior in the American Imagination.* Dissertation, University of Florida, 2012.

Bethune, Albert. Telephone interview by Cynthia Wilson-Graham, January 11, 2014.

Biondi, Joan. *Miami Beach Memories: A Nostalgic Chronicle of Days Gone By.* New York: Globe Pequot, 2006.

Bok, Curtis. Letter to the Directors, The American Foundation. February 5, 1957. http://boktowergardens.org/wp-content/uploads/2011/01/0387_001.pdf.

Brooks, Rev. Dr. Tommy. Interview by Cynthia Wilson-Graham, Ocala, June 19, 2006.

Buculavas, Tina, Peggy Bulger, and Stetson Kennedy. *South Florida Folklife.* Jackson: University Press of Mississippi, 1994.

Carr, Susan Latham. "Ocala's Own Paradise." *Ocala Star Banner,* February 28, 1993.

Carter, Rev. Dr. Mack King. Telephone interview by Cynthia Wilson-Graham, April 10, 2007.

Cheatom, Leon. Interview by Lu Vickers, Ocala, July 29, 2013.

Collins, Oscar. Interview by Lu Vickers, Silver Springs, July 30, 2013.

Cotton, Dr. Clarence. Interview by Lu Vickers, Ocala, July 29, 2013.

Crosby, Naomi. Email interview by Lu Vickers, August 30, 2014.

Crosby, Samuel. Telephone interview by Lu Vickers, December 16, 2013.

Croskey, Carol. Interview by Cynthia Wilson-Graham, Ocala, September 7, 2013.

Curley, James, Sr. Interview by Cynthia Wilson-Graham, Ocala.

Davies, Richard. *Sports in American Life: A History*. Oxford: Wiley-Blackwell, 2012.

Davis, LaRone Taylor. Email interview by Lu Vickers, Orlando, September 17, 2014.

Dickerson, Minnie. "Paradise Park." In *The Struggle for Survival: A Partial History of the Negroes of Marion County, 1865–1976*, ed. Pinkney Woodbury, 48–49. Ocala: Black Historical Association of Marion County, 1977.

Doak, Robin. *The March on Washington: Uniting Against Racism*. Minneapolis: Compass Point Books, 2008.

DuBois, W.E.B. *Black Reconstruction in America: Toward a History of the Part Which Black Folk Played in the Attempt to Reconstruct Democracy in America, 1860–1880*. New Brunswick: Transaction Publishers, 2013.

Faison, David. Interview by Lu Vickers, Silver Springs, July 30, 2013.

Faison, Mayo. Interview by Cynthia Wilson-Graham, Ocala.

Faison, Roosevelt. Interview by Lu Vickers, Silver Springs, July 30, 2013.

Ferguson, Virginia. Interview by Lu Vickers, Ocala, July 29, 2013.

"Florida, the Land of Sunshine, Oranges, and Health." Belmore Florida Land Company, 1885. PALMM. State Library and Archives of Florida. https://archive.org/details/floridalandofsunoobelm.

Flynn, Brenda. Email interview by Lu Vickers, Ocala, June 26, 2014.

Fordham, Edmond. Interview by Lu Vickers, Ocala, July 29, 2013.

Foster, Mark. "In the Face of Jim Crow." *Journal of Negro History* 84, No. 2 (Spring 1999): 130–49.

Goldberg, David. "Greetings from Jim Crow, New Jersey: Contesting the Meaning and Abandonment of Reconstruction in the Public and Commercial Spaces of Asbury Park, 1880–1890." *Concept* 30 (November 2006). http://concept.journals.villanova.edu/article/viewFile/279/242.

Green, Ben. *Before His Time: The Untold Story of Harry T. Moore, America's First Civil Rights Martyr*. Gainesville: University Press of Florida, 2005.

Green, Timothy. Interview by Cynthia Wilson-Graham, Ocala, February 9, 2005, and February 13, 2006.

Green, Victor. *The Negro Traveler's Green Book*. New York: Victor H. Green, 1949.

Haynes, Narvella. Interview by Lu Vickers, Ocala, July 30, 2013.

Hemenway, Robert. *Zora Neale Hurston: A Literary Biography*. Chicago: University of Illinois Press, 1980.

Hollis, Tim. *Glass Bottom Boats* and *Mermaid Tails: Florida's Tourist Springs*. Mechanicsburg, Pa.: Stackpole Books, 2006.

Howard, Walter. *Lynchings: Extralegal Violence in Florida during the 1930s*. Selinsgrove, Pa.: Susquehanna University Press, 1995; iUniverse, 2005.

Hurston, Zora Neale. *Color Struck*. In *Zora Neale Hurston: Collected Plays*, Ed. Jean Lee Cole and Charles Mitchell. New Brunswick: Rutgers University Press, 2008.

———. *Seraph on the Suwannee*. New York: Harper Perennial Modern Classics, 2008.

Jackson, David H. *Booker T. Washington and the Struggle against White Supremacy: The Southern Educational Tours, 1908–1912*. New York: Palgrave MacMillan, 2008.

Jacobs, Johnnye. Interview by Lu Vickers, Tallahassee, February 18, 2014.

Jacobs-Smith, Doris. Interview by Lu Vickers, Tallahassee, February 18, 2014.

Jenkins, Loretta Pompey. Interview by Lu Vickers, Ocala, July 29, 2013.

Jenkins, Whitfield. Interview by Lu Vickers, Ocala, July 29, 2013.

Jones, Henry. Interview by Lu Vickers, Ocala, July 30, 2013.

Jones, Kenneth. Email interview by Lu Vickers, Tallahassee, May 7, 2014.

Jones, Sylvia. Interview by Lu Vickers, Ocala, July 29, 2013.

Karhl, Andrew. *The Land Was Ours: African American Beaches from Jim Crow to the Sunbelt South.* Cambridge: Harvard University Press, 2012.

King, Gilbert. *Devil in the Grove: Thurgood Marshall, the Groveland Boys, and the Dawn of a New America.* New York: Harper Perennial, 2013.

Lake, Luresa. Interview by Lu Vickers, Ocala, July 30, 2013.

Lamb, Chris. *Blackout: The Untold Story of Jackie Robinson's First Spring Training.* Lincoln: Bison Books, 2006.

Lanier, Sidney. *Florida: Its Scenery, Climate, and History. With an account of Charleston, Savannah, Augusta, and Aiken; a chapter for consumptives; various papers on fruit-culture; and a complete hand-book and guide.* Philadelphia: J. B. Lippincott and Company, 1876.

Levine, Lawrence. *Black Culture and Black Consciousness: Afro-American Folk Thought from Slavery to Freedom.* Oxford: Oxford University Press, 1997.

Lewis, Nathaniel "Pepper." Interview by Lu Vickers, Ocala, July 30, 2013.

Lewis, Reginald. Telephone interview by Lu Vickers, September 28, 2014.

Long, Austin. Interview by Cynthia Wilson-Graham, Ocala, April 29, 2006, and February 8, 2015.

Mabry, J. Donald. *World's Finest Beach: A Brief History of the Jacksonville Beaches.* Charleston: History Press, 2010.

Marsh, Willie, and William Crowell. Interview with Nancy Nusz, March 9, 1984. Library Folklife Program, audio recording, Florida Memory Project.

Martin, Richard. *Eternal Spring.* St. Petersburg: Great Outdoors Publishing, 1966.

Maxwell, Bill. "Angry Young Man." *Forum: The Magazine of the Florida Humanities Council* 22, no. 2 (Summer 1999): 8–17.

Maxwell, Bill. Telephone interview by Lu Vickers, June 20, 2014.

McCall, George A. *Letters from the Frontiers.* Philadelphia: J. B. Lippincott and Company, 1868. http://lincoln.lib.niu.edu/cgi-bin/philologic/getobject.pl?c.5118:65.lincoln.

McCarthy, Kevin. *African American Sites in Florida.* Sarasota: Pineapple Press, 2007.

Miller, Dr. Dorsey. Interview by Cynthia Wilson-Graham, Ocala, May 13, 2014.

Monroe, Gary. "The Fate of Silver Springs, Florida's Paradise on Earth." *Lisa Stone Arts.* http://www.lisastonearts.com/gary-monroe-considers-fate-of-silver-springs.html.

Mozert, Bruce. Interview by Lu Vickers, Ocala, July 29, 2013.

Nielsen, Wayne. Email interview by Lu Vickers, May 24, 2014.

Norton, Charles Ledyard. *Handbook of Florida.* New York: Longmans, Green and Company, 1892.

Ott, Eloise Robinson, and Louis Hickman Chazal. *Ocali Country: Kingdom of the Sun*. Ocala: Perry Printing Company, 1966.

"Paradise Park," brochure. By permission of Cynthia Wilson-Graham.

Parker-Warren, Carrie. Email interview by Lu Vickers, September 13, 2014.

Pasteur, Gloria Johnson. Interview by Cynthia Wilson-Graham, Ocala, September 9, 2013; phone interview by Cynthia Wilson-Graham, November 20, 2013.

Perkins, Freddie Lee. Interview by Cynthia Wilson-Graham, Ocala, June 19, 2006, and November 19, 2006.

Perkins, May Vinzant. *Aunt Aggie's Bone Yard: Historic Old Garden of Lake City, Florida*. No publisher, 1953.

Pinkston, Amelia. Interview by Cynthia Wilson-Graham, Ocala, August 25, 2014.

Rackard, David. Telephone interview by Cynthia Wilson-Graham, May 12, 2014, and September 22, 2014.

Raines, McCloud, Jr. Interview by Cynthia Wilson-Graham, Ocala, May 2005.

Ramsey, Leoneade. *The Luffmans* and *Allied Families 1710–1967*. John Williams, 1968.

Ray, Bill "Blue." Interview by Cynthia Wilson-Graham, Ocala, February 9, 2005.

Roundtree, Leroy. Interview by Cynthia Wilson-Graham, Ocala, March 6, 2005.

Rozier, Alice Robinson. Telephone interview by Lu Vickers, October 8, 2014.

Rugh, Susan Sessions. *Are We There Yet? The Golden Age of American Family Vacations*. Lawrence: University Press of Kansas. 2008

Rymer, Russ. *American Beach: A Saga of Race, Wealth, and Memory* New York: Harper Collins, 1998.

Samuel, Edgar. Interview by Cynthia Wilson-Graham, Ocala, October 22, 2007.

Saunders, Dr. Robert W. Sr. Oral history interview by Canter Brown, January 14, 2002. Scholar Commons, University of South Florida. http://scholarcom mons.usf.edu/cgi/viewcontent.cgi?article=1161&context=flstud_oh.

Scott, Dr. Joyce Hope. Email interview by Lu Vickers, September 3, 2014.

Scott, Dr. Joyce Hope. "Official Language, Unofficial Reality: Acquiring Bilingual, Bicultural Fluency in a Segregated Southern Town." In *The Real Ebonics Debate: Power, Language, and the Education of African-American Children*, ed. Lisa Delpit and Theresa Perrs, 189–90, 194–95. Boston: Beacon Press, 1998.

"Silver Springs Daylight Route," brochure. By permission of Lu Vickers.

Smith, Elaine. *Mary McLeod Bethune and the National Council of Negro Women, Pursuing a True and Unfettered Democracy*. Tuscaloosa: Alabama State University, 2003.

Stearns, Marshall Winslow, and Jean Stearns. *Jazz Dance: The Story of American Vernacular Dance*. New York: Da Capo Press, 1968.

Stevenson, L. C. Interview by Cynthia Wilson-Graham, Ocala, August 28, 2006, and May 12, 2014.

Stone, Robert. *Sacred Steel: Inside an African American Steel Guitar Tradition*. Urbana: University of Illinois Press, 2010.

Stowe, Harriet Beecher. "A Sail into Fairyland." *The Christian World Magazine*, 1873; Google eBook.

Tillman, Vivian Vereen. Interview by Lu Vickers, Ocala, July 29, 2013.

Urlin, Ethel. *Dancing Ancient and Modern*. New York: D. Appleton and Company, 1912.

Vereen, Brenda. Interview by Lu Vickers, Ocala, July 30, 2013.

Vereen-Turner, Arizona. Interview by Lu Vickers, Ocala, July 30, 2013.

Walker, Vanessa Siddle. *Their Highest Potential: An African American School Community in the Segregated South*. Chapel Hill: University of North Carolina Press, 2006.

West, Patsy. *The Enduring Seminoles: From Alligator Wrestling to Ecotourism*. Gainesville: University Press of Florida, 1998.

Whitehead, Colson. *Sag Harbor*. New York: Anchor, 2010.

Williams, Riley. Interview by Lu Vickers, Ocala, July 30, 2013.

Williams, Mary Carolyn. Interview by Cynthia Wilson-Graham, Ocala.

Wilson, Jon, and Rosalie Peck. *St. Petersburg's Historic 22nd Street South*. Charleston: History Press, 2006.

Wiltse, Jeff. *Contested Waters: A Social History of Swimming Pools in America*. Chapel Hill: University of North Carolina Press, 2010.

Woodbury, Pinkney. *The Struggle for Survival: A Partial History of the Negroes of Marion County, 1865–1976*. Ocala: Black Historical Association of Marion County, 1977.

Woodward, C. Vann. T*he Strange Career of Jim Crow*. Oxford: Oxford University Press. 2001.

Index

LU VICKERS was awarded a National Endowment for the Arts Fellowship for fiction in 2014. She has also received three Individual Artists Fellowships from the Florida Arts Council. She is the author of *Breathing Underwater*, a novel, and three nonfiction books: *Weeki Wachee: City of Mermaids*; *Cypress Gardens: America's Tropical Wonderland*; and with Bonnie Georgiadis, *Weekee Wachee Mermaids: Thirty Years of Underwater Photography*.

CYNTHIA WILSON-GRAHAM is an independent photographer and founder of Helping Hands Photography and Desktop Publishing Company. She has freelanced for the *Ocala Star Banner*, *Ocala Magazine*, and *UNITE Magazine*. She currently is first vice president of the Marion County Chapter of the NAACP and a member of the Region IV Head Start Association Board of Directors, Silver Springs Alliance, and Friends of Silver Springs State Park; she is an alumna of Head Start, Focus on Leadership, and Leadership Ocala/Marion.